"By the time you finish *Reconciling Places*, many pages will be dog-eared for future reference. Hoffman is not an armchair theologian pontificating ideas that work in theory alone; he's a tested, bridge-building disciple who has embodied reconciliation with his life and ministry."

—**Matthew D. Kim**, author of *Preaching with Cultural Intelligence*

"*Reconciling Places* is a well-written and engaging discussion about building bridges across differences. Paul Hoffman guides his readers through ideas and stories and examples of what it means to do just that—to span the divide in our thinking and ultimately in our communities, to act biblically, theologically, Christianly through prayer, by the words we use with each other, and by forming connections with other reconcilers."

—**Scott M. Gibson**, David E. Garland Professor of Preaching, George W. Truett Theological Seminary, Baylor University

"Paul challenges you to go deeper and look within yourself in his book *Reconciling Places*. These are not merely written words on a piece of paper but a man of faith who has prayed many years not only to embrace reconciliation but lived it out as a personal testimony in Jesus Christ. My highest recommendation."

—**Stephen A. Robinson**, author of *Mega-Small Church*

"In a time of great confusion, disorientation, and division, how can we find our place in this world and in God's plan for Earth? This book is a foundational starting point, especially for those drawn to justice, reconciliation, and peacemaking efforts. . . . The message of this book is more relevant today than any other time in history. We need a generation of reconcilers and peacemakers to arise as never before."

—**Tom and Kate Hess**, Jerusalem House of Prayer for All Nations, Mount of Olives

"In this book Paul Hoffman takes readers on a theological journey, offering examples of speaking into urban spaces as a reconciled reconciler. Fleshing out theology into deeper understandings of the story of God-at-work in the lives of real people, it is earthed in lived examples of his experiences of reconciliation as a pastor and leader. Widening theological ideas, engaging with research, giving voice to the breadth of this field, this book is readable but deep, encouraging us to see the world (and church) newly, change our practice, be challenged in our thinking, and reflect more of the very nature of God."

—**Deirdre Brower Latz**, Principal and Senior Lecturer in Pastoral and Social Theology, Nazarene Theological College

"If you care about peace, reconciliation, healing, and community building, *Reconciling Places* is for you. . . . Hoffman demonstrates God's great desire to build a peaceful, unified community that is delivered from hostility, suspicion, and hatred that separates. *Reconciling Places* is not just another academic work. The words you read in this book have been lived. First by Jesus our Savior, but secondly by the author whose words are matched by his character. . . . Paul is the real deal and this book is the real thing. I highly recommend it!"

—**Thomas L. Crawford**, Executive Director of Evangelical Friends Church-Eastern Region

Reconciling Places

Reconciling Places

How to Bridge the Chasms in our Communities

Paul A. Hoffman

FOREWORD BY
J. R. Woodward

CASCADE *Books* • Eugene, Oregon

RECONCILING PLACES
How to Bridge the Chasms in our Communities

Cascade Books
An Imprint of Wipf and Stock Publishers
199 W. 8th Ave., Suite 3
Eugene, OR 97401

www.wipfandstock.com

PAPERBACK ISBN: 978-1-5326-5122-9
HARDCOVER ISBN: 978-1-5326-5123-6
EBOOK ISBN: 978-1-5326-5124-3

Cataloguing-in-Publication data:

Names: Hoffman, Paul A., author. | Woodward, J. R., foreword.

Title: Reconciling places: how to bridge the chasms in our communities / by Paul A. Hoffman; foreword by J. R. Woodward.

Description: Eugene, OR: Cascade Books, 2020 | Includes bibliographical references.

Identifiers: ISBN 978-1-5326-5122-9 (paperback) | ISBN 978-1-5326-5123-6 (hardcover) | ISBN 978-1-5326-5124-3 (ebook)

Subjects: LCSH: Reconciliation—Religious aspects—Christianity. | Christianity and justice. | Sacred space.

Classification: BT738.27 .H50 2020 (print) | BT738.27 (ebook)

Manufactured in the U.S.A.   08/11/20

To the people of
Evangelical Friends Church of Newport,
past, present, and future:
you have taught me far more than
I have taught you.
For this I remain deeply humbled and grateful.

Contents

Foreword

ONE WAY TO COMPREHEND the increasing polarization in our world is by understanding the competing ideologies in America today. There is "nationalism" or "white nationalism" on one end and "progressive liberalism" on the other. Both are ideologies and both are idols as well. David Koyzis, in his book *Political Visions & Illusions*, makes a solid case that ideology is idolatry because an ideology has its own account of sin and redemption. It has its own soteriology, its own eschatology, its own *telos*. Like any idol, every ideology seeks ultimate allegiance and promises to save people from real or perceived fear. To that end, ideology causes blindness and deafness. Often when people are captive to ideology, their ability to listen to or view something from a different perspective is limited or nonexistent.

This blindness and deafness happen not only to people outside the faith but also to those who are seeking to follow Jesus. The Gospel of Mark often portrays the disciples as blind and deaf to *who* Jesus was and *what* his mission was truly about. It is no accident that at the center of the Gospel of Mark (7:31—9:30) reside stories of Jesus healing the sight of two different men, and in the middle Jesus casts out a deaf and dumb spirit.

Sight is an important metaphor for Mark, and the healing of one of the blind men in two stages (Mark 8:22–26) indicates the confused state of the disciples. It is directly after this that Jesus asks the disciples, "Who do you say that I am?" While Peter responded with insight, it wasn't long before Jesus rebuked him sharply, saying, "Get behind me, Satan," indicating his insight was followed by a significant blind spot.

The Apostle Paul said that he saw through a mirror dimly (1 Cor 13:12). Those with wisdom recognize that there is only One who sees truth objectively. For the rest of us, our point of view is shaped by the point from which we view the world. Our context, where we stand geographically, sociologically, economically, biologically, and autobiographically, shapes how we view reality. In the parable of the sower the only variable is the location of the soil. The sower and seed are the same. The location of the soil determines the response. Likewise, the reigning ideology of where we live tends to hold us captive and in bondage to idolatry, which in turn leads to dehumanizing others. The ecology of our heart is not neutral; it is deeply shaped and often misshaped by socialization in a polarized world.

The truth we seek is not found in ideology. It is found in a person, the great Reconciler of the world—Jesus Christ. Jesus destroyed the wall of hostility between those who have been divided by the socialization processes of this world (Eph 2:14–18). Jesus has taken the hostility, animosity, and suspicion between people who are captive to ideology, and through his death and resurrection, he has created one new humanity. Now together, as this one new humanity, we can seek first his kingdom and his righteousness (Matt 6:33).

Ideology, like all idols, seeks full devotion from those it holds captive so that, in time, citizenship of country replaces discipleship to Christ, or submission to political correctness replaces our love for true freedom. Submission to ideology erects walls of hostility between people. Jesus was and is good at destroying walls and building bridges. In fact, Jesus became the ultimate bridge by his willingness to die for his friends and his enemies.

Paul Hoffman, in *Reconciling Places*, captures the heart of the good news of Jesus by helping us to become bridge builders. One of the beautiful contributions that Hoffman makes in this book is how he tells the story of God. Instead of using the common story line of creation, fall, redemption, and consummation, he frames the story relationally. Drawing on the fact that in the beginning was community, Hoffman puts reconciliation at the center of what our triune God is doing in this world. He reminds us that the Creator of this good world is reconciling us not just to himself but to each other, within ourselves, and with all of creation. The good news that gives us hope in our polarized world is the recognition that Christ came "to reconcile all things to himself, whether things on earth or things in heaven, by making peace through his blood, shed on the cross" (Col 1:20). Our ultimate hope is in our triune God's ability to bring about new creation. It is a hope that is based on the love of the Father, the faithfulness of the Son, and the power of the Holy Spirit.

Hoffman is wise in reminding us that if we are to be bridge builders we must count the cost, as this work is not for the fainthearted. Seeking to be reconcilers is excruciating and demanding work. Hoffman, after recognizing the importance of the places we dwell, gives us the foundation and substructure of bridge building before diving into concrete reconciliation practices. He does this because he recognizes that if we are going to have endurance in our reconciliation practices, our practices must be constructed on a foundation that allows us to move forward with faith, hope, and love.

I've had the pleasure of getting to know Paul, as we were simultaneously pursuing our PhDs at the University of Manchester (UK). When spending time with him, I quickly picked up that this theme of reconciliation flows from his heart. As you read this book, you will realize that *Reconciling Places* is not just a theoretical journey for Paul; it is a journey that he is living out. What makes this book come alive for me is getting a peek at how God was shaping this life message in Paul from the time he was young to this very day. My own heart has been encouraged in reading this book by seeing his pursuit of reconciliation in the concrete places he dwells. Seeing him step out in faith by bringing people and churches together to take a public stand against racism lifted my heart. I was encouraged by his realism and his willingness to share both his victories and defeats. For not only is the work of reconciliation costly; it is messy.

The fact is that we are all a part of some narrative, and the story we live in shapes the script we write day-to-day. What story are you living in? How does that story shape your relationships with your family and friends, or even better, how does that story shape how you treat your enemies? Does the story you live in draw you to our triune God and his work of reconciliation in our world? Does the story in which you live help you experience constructive transformation in your life and in the lives of others? When you imagine the future, do you have a sense of hope or despair?

As you start to read this book, you will soon see what gives Hoffman hope. The first chapter is devoted to place—the city and towns in which we live. This significance of place speaks to Hoffman's understanding of incarnation. He doesn't want us to see the places we live with just ordinary eyes. Within the first chapter, he gives us *four lenses* to broaden our view of place. Through these lenses we appreciate the beauty and brokenness of the built environment but we are also reminded of God's commitment to new creation through the lens of eschatology. He threads this eschatological lens throughout the book. For as we reflect on God's future, a renewed heaven and earth, and let it shape our sense of calling, we can live sacramentally in the neighborhoods to which God has sent us, writing a new future for our cities and for the world by anticipating his future in the present. In this way, we become people who live with a sustaining faith, a stubborn hope, and a sacrificial love. Ideology doesn't produce this kind of life. But if we seek God first, and desire to see his kingdom and righteousness become more manifest in our neighborhoods, we will become peacemakers, demonstrating that we are children of God.

J. R. Woodward

Seattle, Washington
Epiphany 2020

Preface

I WAS IN THE process of making the final edits for this book (which I started writing in February 2018) when a national powder keg exploded. On May 25, 2020, came the devastating news of the tragic and immoral death of George Floyd at the hands of four Minneapolis police officers. The nine agonizing minutes that officer Derek Chauvin pressed his knee into Mr. Floyd's neck—effectively killing him—were caught on camera and have been viewed by millions of people across the world. When I watched the video, I experienced a soul-shattering grief and wept.

Numerous plumes of righteous anger and angst have erupted from cities across the United States (and the globe), expressed in the form of protests (the vast majority being peaceful) along with some incidents of rioting, looting, and arson.

The death of Mr. Floyd has brought us to an undeniable inflection point. To be sure, our national crisis has been precipitated by multiple factors, including: a) as we approach a consequential presidential election (November 2020), you can feel the toxicity infusing our political-partisan environment intensifying, b) due to the COVID-19 pandemic, over 100,000 Americans have died and tens of millions are unemployed or underemployed, c) surveys indicate more than one-third of people are wrestling with anxiety and depression,[1] and d) thousands of churches are struggling with the pressures and logistics related to regathering for live worship services.

How did I respond? On June 1, I was invited to participate in a prayer vigil for racial justice in honor and memory of George Floyd at Liberty Square in Newport, Rhode Island, organized by the NAACP Newport (Rhode Island) Branch. Everything about the rally felt significant, unifying, and healing. Along with the rally organizers—including clergy and

---

1. Galvin, "Coronavirus Survey," *US News & World Report*, May 27, 2020. https://www.usnews.com/news/healthiest-communities/articles/2020-05-27/one-third-of-us-adults-have-signs-of-depression-anxiety-during-pandemic.

government officials—I shared my heart (testified) and led the crowd in prayer.

To me, this event beautifully captured the essence of the *reconciling places* model presented in this book. If you would like to gain a sense of what occurred, I strongly encourage you to watch the fifty-six-minute video of the rally,[2] read the news coverage,[3] and check out my personal reflections.[4]

In the final analysis, while the reconciling work of the cross is finished, our work as God's reconcilers is not yet done.

Paul Hoffman

June 5, 2020

2. Belmore, "NAACP Prayer Vigil," *Whatsupnewp*, June 1, 2020. https://whatsupnewp.com/2020/06/video-naacp-prayer-vigil-for-racial-justice-held-in-newport/.

3. Damon, "Peaceful vigil," *Newport Daily News*, June 1, 2020. https://www.newportri.com/news/20200601/peaceful-vigil-held-in-newport-in-wake-of-george-floydrsquos-killing.

4. Hoffman, "A Way Forward," *Newport This Week*, June 4, 2020. https://www.newportthisweek.com/articles/a-way-forward/?fbclid=IwAR2PI8xGj937dewvRE3OrQdiecXF5DnpUm6D6bTa6fNB3RdP1v8fVl_6FKk; Hoffman and Kim, "Four Ways Church Leaders Can Inspire Racial Healing," Influence Magazine, June 10, 2020. https://influencemagazine.com/en/Practice/Four-Ways-Church-Leaders-Can-Inspire-Racial-Healing; Hoffman, "Activism 101: How Churches Can Respond to the Death of George Floyd," ChurchLeaders, June 15, 2020. https://churchleaders.com/outreach-missions/outreach-missions-articles/377212-activism-101-how-churches-can-respond-to-the-death-of-george-floyd.html.

Standing on the left: Pastor Steve Robinson. Standing on Steve's right, holding the microphone, Pastor Paul Hoffman. For over fourteen years, we have been best friends and co-laborers in the ministry of reconciliation. (Photograph courtesy of Ryan Belmore, *Whatsupnewp*.)

Acknowledgments

THERE ARE COPIOUS PEOPLE to thank for their profound contributions to this book. First, I praise and honor the triune God: Father, Son, and Holy Spirit for creating me, regenerating me, and providing me with the gifts, abilities, experience, training, passions, empowerment, and determination to run this race. My deepest desire is to glorify you in my life, ministry, and writing.

To Albert and Kellie Fassbender: I cannot begin to thank you enough for your invaluable input and editing prowess (both this book and my PhD thesis!).

To Trip Wolfskehl: thanks for the ongoing encouragement and for providing the Newport Bridge graphic. You are a great friend.

To Drew Harris and Trisha Bruce: thank you for compiling the bibliography.

To Stephen Robinson: you have been a friend, mentor, and co-laborer. I praise God for your influence over my life and ministry.

To my parents and siblings: Mom, Dad, Kate, Melissa, Caleb, and Will. Thanks for your support and prayers. Ubuntu.

To the leaders and people of EFC: thank you for putting up with your intermittently distracted pastor. This book is dedicated to you.

To my wife Autumn, and sons, Landon and Kelan: you mean more to me than I can ever express. You inspire me to write. I am deeply grateful for your patience and granting me the freedom to toil in this way.

Thank you Cascade Books and my editor Rodney Clapp for believing in me and making this book possible.

Introduction: Our Place— the Divided States of America

ON FRIDAY MORNING, JULY 8, 2016, I awoke to the troubling news on my iPhone. Tears initiated an unauthorized launch sequence in my eyes, a rare and unwelcome occurrence for a man of stoic roots—Midwestern and German to be exact. A swirl of emotions collided within me: sadness, righteous anger, fear, and helplessness. The phrase "Enough is enough!" ricocheted around my mind.

Overnight, a sniper had shot twelve law enforcement officers in downtown Dallas, Texas. Five of these public servants died. The cruel irony was that they were supporting a peaceful protest in response to two deaths—only days earlier—involving altercations with police. On Tuesday, July 5, Alton Sterling, a thirty-seven-year-old black male, was shot in Baton Rouge, Louisiana, outside a convenience store. Then on Wednesday, July 6, officer Jeronimo Yanez, during a seemingly routine traffic stop outside Saint Paul, Minnesota, shot Philando Castile, a young black male. Castile's girlfriend, Diamond Reynolds, streamed the aftermath on Facebook Live. Viewers watched Philando fall unconscious as he slowly bled to death. I was horrified to hear Reynolds's four-year-old daughter, Dae'Anna, comfort her mother while attempting to process this tragic event: "It's OK, Mommy . . . it's OK, I'm right here with you. . . . Mom, please stop cussing and scream-ing 'cause I don't want you to get shooted. . . . I wish this town was safer. I don't want it to be like this anymore."[1]

This little girl was not alone in her fear and confusion. On Friday, July 8, the Bahamas issued a travel advisory to Bahamians entering the United States: "Young males are asked to exercise extreme caution in affected cit-ies in their interactions with the police. Do not be confrontational and

---

1. Etehad, "'I Don't Want You to Get Shooted.'"

cooperate."[2] For many Americans this news felt surreal: Since when did tourists need to fear to vacation in the United States?

I gathered my emotions, paced my bedroom floor, and passionately prayed. I asked God for wisdom because to do nothing seemed wrong. Finally, I told my wife I wanted to call an impromptu prayer meeting at noon in front of Newport (Rhode Island) City Hall. I started to compose a text message to some of my pastor friends in the area, inviting them to join me. Then I stopped: a different tone was required. I rewrote the text. Instead of making a tentative appeal, I notified them I was following God's prompting and implored them to join me at our city center and publicly pray for our broken hearts and divided nation. Then I posted a statement on my Facebook account, calling for all people of faith and goodwill to gather with us and pray, and if not, to stop and pray at noon wherever they were. Ryan Belmore, the founder of Whatsupnewp.com (a hub of all things Newport), noticed my plea, and wrote a story and posted it on his popular website. Simultaneously, two sisters, Paula and Marie, our church's[3] public relations virtuosos, reached out to local media to spread the news. All of a sudden, friends and parishioners who planned to attend the rally inundated me with private messages and text messages, some offering support, others confirming details. People felt a compelling desire to connect, and this meeting was catching fire fast.

Around 11:45, I jumped on my bike and pedaled the two miles to city hall. A crowd was forming. By about 12:05, over fifty people had gathered in the plaza in front of the imposing granite building. Far from my usual pastoral tribe of middle-aged, mostly white men, I beheld a cross section of Newport itself: elementary kids, preteens, soccer moms, retirees; those wearing designer sunglasses next to young men sporting baggy T-shirts from Walmart; black, white, brown, and biracial faces from (we estimated) ten local churches. Multiple TV stations and newspaper reporters clamored to interview the attendees.

I called the meeting to order, stating we had gathered in response to the tragic events in Baton Rouge, Saint Paul, and Dallas. Our country was hurting. People were scared. We had come together to pray because prayer makes a difference—it changes our hearts, if not always our circumstances. It

---

2. Government of the Bahamas, "Ministry of Foreign Affairs."

3. Please note that throughout the book I will follow the Apostles' Creed and capitalize "Church" when referring to the Church universal. I will use "church" to refer to a local church or congregation.

unites people in powerful ways. Anyone who wants to pray can pray: silently, out loud, through song, in any way he or she feels led.

And pray we did: for over an hour perfect strangers staged an impromptu revival meeting. They held hands, poured out their hearts in prayer, wept, sang, laughed, cheered, and shouted "Amen!" The reporters stood fixated and kept filming to the very end. Afterward, many of the attendees hung around, introduced themselves to each another, exchanged cell numbers (or friend requests), and headed for local coffee shops to continue their conversations.

I was amazed: things like this don't often occur in Rhode Island or New England, especially in public spaces. We see ourselves as the "frozen chosen," proud for being curmudgeonly, thrifty, independent, intellectual, and perhaps even just a little bit superior.

But that day rebutted the naysayers. Yes, America and many parts of the world are deeply polarized by issues of race, class, politics, economics, gender, education, location, and legal status, to name a few. Our divisions are real and grave and so must be addressed. However, so many of us are hungry to connect in meaningful and generous ways that seek to bridge the barriers separating us. From this, I surmise people are still attracted to good news, to a positive narrative: a story of hope that overcomes despair, of love that conquers hate, of a unity that does not impose uniformity but respects our differences. Americans are longing for this story to animate solutions that are constructive rather than destructive, to dignify and uplift rather than debase and tear down.

We hunger for a vision of reconciliation, don't we? And so the question is "how do we, together, bridge the chasms in our communities?" Or more pointedly, "how do we become and grow as reconcilers?"

A white boy from Portland, Maine: My journey to the intersection of reconciliation and place

My journey as a passionate, albeit imperfect, advocate for reconciliation, unity, and justice makes me chuckle because it was at first inauspicious. I was born ten weeks premature on February 8, 1977, at Fletcher-Allen Hospital, the teaching hospital of the University of Vermont. I weighed just two pounds, thirteen ounces. The doctors told my parents the odds of my survival were low, owing to my mother's preeclampsia and birth complications. Kurt and Linda Hoffman prayed and believed their son had a purpose. After all, they named him after the apostle of New Testament fame (thanks, Mom and Dad, for setting unrealistically high expectations!). By God's grace, I survived and started to grow and thrive: the expedition commenced.

As life marched forward, my parents added my two sisters into the Hoffman family. Unfortunately, shortly after my younger sister was born, my parents divorced. My mother won primary custody of us and took a teaching job in Skowhegan, Maine. Second grade was a miserable year: I was the new kid in a small mill town where nobody new arrived and even fewer left. I recall during recess, a few of the children on the playground picked on me for being undersized (ironically the name "Paul" means "humble" or "small") and poor. One experience painfully sticks out. As we approached the school's annual Christmas gift exchange, my family lacked enough spare money to buy a new gift for my Secret Santa. So my mother and I made the best of a challenging situation: we wrapped a used Matchbox car discovered during a recent foray to a yard sale and spent hours crafting a homemade Santa sleigh out of candy canes, construction paper, stickers, and glitter. I thought it was a masterpiece. My classmate thought otherwise: upon opening the gifts, his brow furled and his lips curled in partially veiled incredulity and disgust: "Is this Matchbox car used? What's this thing you made?" I remember my cheeks burning as waves of shame, rejection, and humiliation swept over me. It was the first time I learned that difference—whether intentionally or unintentionally—might be used to degrade and dehumanize others. In this case, my perceived poverty made me inferior. I was thankful that at the end of the school year we relocated to Orono, Maine.

During my third and fourth grade years at Asa Adams Elementary School, I had two more experiences regarding "difference" that would further tilt the trajectory of my life toward reconciliation. The first centered on a schoolmate named Salvador Casañas Diaz, my first-ever best friend. Salvador (Sal) and I would go on wild adventures, spending countless hours racing Huffy BMX bikes around our idyllic college town, collecting bottles from the sidewalks and trash cans and then refunding them for a few dollars so we could buy bubble gum, gumdrops, and lollipops. But the biggest adventure took place indoors. I will never forget the first time I entered Sal's apartment. The space was infused with the pungent scent of rice and beans simmering in a pot, the sound of Puerto Rican salsa music blaring from a boom box, and the strange intonations and cadences of Spanish floating about as his relatives bantered among themselves. I was intrigued: Sal's world was unique and foreign. A new realization struck me: not every person ate the same food, spoke the same language, or listened to Casey Kasem's Top Forty radio countdown. Different could be beautiful. I didn't know it then, but my first cross-cultural (interracial) friendship would open me to the possibility and pursuit of many others in the years to come.

A second transformative event involved Ryan Grant (not his real name), a school bully who happened to be older and bigger than me. One Saturday Sal and I raced our bikes to the playground at Asa Adams. We discovered a space devoid of children except for Ryan and his buddy pushing their girlfriends on the tire swings. He did not approve of our interrupting his private rendezvous and uncouthly demanded we leave immediately. Likewise, Sal and I did not appreciate his monopolizing this public space. We exchanged words, and he chased us off the playground. Sal and I fled the scene intoxicated by a combination of fear, anger, and adrenaline. This war wasn't over. Shortly after that, I heard a rumor Ryan was visiting a friend at my apartment complex. I hopped onto my bike and sped to the area of the alleged sighting. It was he. If I recall correctly—and to my shame—I taunted him. Ryan cast a cold glare at me, I panicked, and fled the scene. Upon my entry into our apartment, my father quickly ascertained his son was frantically escaping conflict with a bully. With a piercing ferocity, Dad stared into my eyes and declared, "You can't run away from that! You can't let someone intimidate you. You must stand up for yourself." With my weak legs trembling, Dad marched me outside to the front of our building, where Ryan was eagerly waiting. Without delay, Ryan and I began shoving each other, which quickly devolved into a muddy wrestling match. I could hear my father goading Ryan to "stand up and fight like a man." Again, I tried to escape to the safe confines of my apartment, but Kurt Hoffman blocked me and said: "Go back, Son." I am told (in truth I hardly remember a whit about my first and, at present, only fistfight) I punched Ryan in the face two times, and apparently shocked that I fought back, he staggered off.

When pondering that incident, I struggle with my role in the conflict. Although Ryan was older and bigger (did I mention the size of Dwayne "The Rock" Johnson!?) and thus our interactions were marked by a power differential, I did nothing to bridge that chasm. I failed to initiate a conversation with Ryan or ask my Dad to referee one. I know conflict is inevitable: it's a consequence of human beings attempting to share limited resources and overlapping spaces. But when confronting power, what means should we deploy before physical force is brought to bear? How does reconciling work when an opponent is violent or unreasonable?

With the benefit of hindsight, I find it fascinating that as a young child I was learning that class, race, gender, and power shape our differences—how we interpret them and respond to them. I also gleaned there exists, at the very least, three approaches to engaging difference: degradation, appreciation, and confrontation.

Consequently, these experiences catalyzed a lifelong quest to discover how I can join with others (including people of faith, practicing Christians, theology students, and ministry/nongovernment organization [NGO] leaders), to constructively address the differences in our homes, workplaces, churches, communities, and nation. Recently, four areas of my life have coalesced during this pursuit: my Christian faith, extensive world travel,[4] my work as a pastor embedded in a particular place, and my doctoral studies in the areas of practical theology and urban mission. These factors have birthed a fresh model called *reconciling places*, which sits at the intersection of two critical ideas. *Reconciling* encourages Christians to live into their calling and identity as "peacemakers":[5] those who intentionally build bridges across ethnicity (race), class, and sex (gender) differences.[6] *Place* refers to the embracing of one's home, locale, or neighborhood, a particular social and cultural location. It is to be fully present, rooted, and embodied within a specific longitude and latitude.

It must be said I come to you neither as an expert nor a hero. My desire is to serve as a guide on your reconciling journey. I've gathered some experiences and principles along my own voyage that I'd like to share that may assist you in learning about and practicing reconciling as an identity and way of being. It seems you are reading this book because you care deeply about the challenges besetting us, like globalization, political rancor, war, climate change, wealth and income inequality, and the many "isms" we face—classism, racism, sexism, etc. And rather than contributing to our problems, you want to work for solutions.

---

4. Thirty-three countries, and counting, located in the Caribbean, Europe, Africa, Asia, and the Middle East.

5. Matt 5:9.

6. I call this the "Gal 3:28 triad"—more on this in chapter 1.

The importance of refreshing an ancient narrative during troubled times

As a pastor and practical theologian, I believe we gain insight into our divides and discover constructive solutions to our problems by returning to a biblical narrative. If used as a lens, it could help Christians like you and me (and perhaps others) comprehend our world through a frame that faithfully aligns with some of the ways the triune God views and acts within the created order. More to the point, theologians have suggested, "the Bible as a whole tells a story, in some sense a single story."[7] Missiologist Tim Tennent and Pastor Timothy Keller indicate the Bible depicts a story of creation, fall, redemption, and restoration.[8] While this is good so far as it goes, I think it's more complete when presented in five movements: Creator, first creation, alienation, reconciliation, and final creation. If fully understood, this account provides several enlightening perspectives, including these two:

- Reminding people of faith, it's best—and biblically accurate, I would argue—to view their lives, and history itself, through the lens of a single story: that through Jesus Christ, God the Father seeks to "reconcile to himself all things"[9] by the power of the Holy Spirit.[10] This challenges Christians to enter into some uncomfortable tensions. While the triune God is superintending the reconciling process, for us, it appears messy and alinear. In the face of sin and brokenness, however, followers of Jesus can maintain a sense of purpose, agency, and responsibility because we are joining God on his mission, which thankfully is not entirely dependent on us.

- We start to comprehend and appreciate the profound relationality of God and interconnectedness with his world. After all, the triune God is a relational being interacting within himself[11] and outside himself with creation.[12]

7. Bauckham, *Bible and Mission*, 11–12. This group includes missiologists Michael Goheen and Christopher Wright—more on this in chapter 2.

8. Tennent, *Invitation to World Missions*, 105; Keller, *Center Church*, 43.

9. Col 1:20.

10. A note about pronouns: throughout the book I refer to God or members of the Godhead using "he" or "his." I do this primarily for internal consistency with quotations and Scripture. It is not intended to promote androcentrism.

11. Theologians call this the "immanent Trinity."

12. Theologians call this the "economic Trinity."

If you are willing to embrace the theology of reconciliation offered here, I believe you will be equipped to act as reconcilers who build bridges in your context, whether you inhabit cities, suburbs, exurbs, or rural areas. This book, then, aims to help Christian leaders and students act as peacemakers by providing several tools. One is helping them exegete and reflect on the promises and perils of their communities (their unique "places"). Another is to identify the particular ways race, class, and sex (gender) are flash points in their locales, owing, in no small measure, to partisan politics' and social media's magnifying and warping difference (which is God-given and beautiful) and turning it into divides.

These ideas and practices are worth the fight. I know, because I am living this *reconciling places* model in my current home of Newport County, Rhode Island. Alongside the church I lead, Evangelical Friends Church of Newport, I regularly forge local partnerships with people across racial (ethnic), class, and sex (gender) chasms—you'll hear more about these as we go. I believe our community is slowly but surely coming together in the process—that is, if the feedback I am receiving from civic, nonprofit, and religious sources is correct. Indeed life cannot be reduced to neat and tidy boxes, encapsulated by statistics, results, and upward or downward line graphs. Pragmatic and technocratic approaches to life, those that presume impersonal progress leading to never-ceasing prosperity, do not ring true for many of us. These methods are discordant with the messiness we are experiencing as we adventure into the twenty-first century.

In fact, I believe God is raising up a new generation. Many younger Christians are deeply concerned about the polarizing debates in American society. They have soured on partisan rancor, religious polemics, materialistic greed, and wasteful consumption. However, they are hopeful activists with a sensitive social conscience who care passionately about unity without uniformity, respect for diversity, social justice, wise stewardship, and reconciliation. They desire to foster authentic, meaningful, and constructive conversations that lead to practical solutions. This book exists partly to offer a framework for putting their passions and efforts to good use.

Scouting the journey ahead

Let's map out the path going forward. Chapter 1, "Your Place," challenges the reader to recognize the uniqueness and importance of her setting. This motivates her to view and interpret her community with fresh eyes to see its brokenness and beauty. It is helpful to analyze one's location by appropriating a dialectical theology of place. That is, each place reveals aspects of Babylon (alienation) and the New Jerusalem (reconciliation)—both are present and must be identified to obtain a clear understanding. Furthermore, chances are that politics and social media exploit ethnicity, class, and sex to further the existing divisions in each community. With this in mind, the Christian, and her faith family can identity their place's painful rifts in order to collaborate with others to build bridges. Along the way, I will include reflections on these dynamics based on the places I have lived: Portland (Maine), Boston, Jerusalem, Denver, Newport, and Manchester (UK).

Chapter 2 is called "The Foundation: The Relational Nature of the Trinity." As the book's subtitle is "How to Bridge the Chasms in our Communities," in this chapter I will start unpacking the crowning analogy of reconciling as building bridges across difference. Engineers tell us most bridges are composed of three major sections: the foundation, substructure, and superstructure.[13] All three areas are interconnected and necessary for a bridge to function properly. Likewise, each section represents a vital theological category required to construct a reconciling place: the relational nature of the Trinity (foundation), reconciling theology (substructure), and reconciling practices (superstructure).

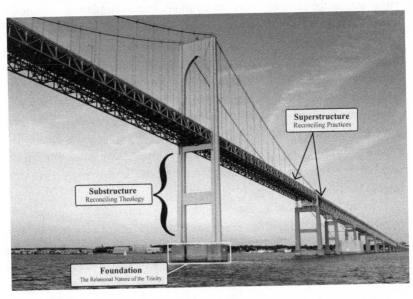

13. History of Bridges, "Structure, Components and Parts of Bridge."

Reconciliation starts with the foundation of the character of the Trinity. One way Christians can better comprehend the triune God is if they read Scripture through a particular lens, what I call a "relational narrative." This lens helps us recognize the reconciling DNA inherent in God's being. I suggest it opens our eyes to see the relational nature of God: both the way God relates facing inward (to himself internally) and facing outward (externally to the world). Reconciling is rooted in the character and personhood of the triune God and his relationship with the created order.

In chapter 3, "The Substructure: Reconciling Theology," I outline the four great theological equalizers: the *imago Dei,* human sinfulness and the brokenness of creation, the vast atoning love of Jesus Christ, and his final judgment. The equality among the persons of God lays the foundation for human equality. With these commitments established, I highlight a few key bonding agents that are needed to hold the reconciling bridge together.

Chapter 4, "The Superstructure: Reconciling Practices," offers the reader actionable ways she can apply the reconciling places model. I challenge Christians to engage in reconciling prayer, reconciling rhetoric, and reconciling communities/coalitions. Because reconciling is so hard, Christians need to be connected to the heart and priorities of God. Prayer is their power source. Prayer shapes a repentant rhetoric. Christians forgo strident language amidst the blare of Twitter rants and political sound bites. Reconcilers pursue face-to-face (incarnational) conversations rather than Facade-Book (disembodied through social media) ones. Moreover, reconcilers "speak the truth in love" (Eph 4:15) while avoiding "two particularly destructive forms of speech: the hurtful insult and the conversation stopper."[14] Our words and tone matter when it comes to reconciling. Finally, the person (and community) committed to reconciling will construct diverse coalitions that focus more on common goals than differences when engaging social issues. This entails embracing two overlapping convictions: "Unity is *not* uniformity" and "We are better together." These three concepts lead reconcilers to work toward the total flourishing of all our places.

In the concluding chapter, I recount organizing another prayer rally in the face of national unrest, then recast Martin Luther King Jr.'s "Beloved Community" for our day and age. I end with a reconciling commission: a dream that my two sons, Landon and Kelan, will join others, including generations to come, in embodying reconciliation, whatever the longitude and latitude in which they invest their lives.

---

14. Inazu, *Confident Pluralism*, 96.

A final disclaimer

As an academically trained practical theologian, I am acutely aware of my limitations, liabilities, and privileged position. Simply put, this book is written from a particular perspective: I am an American white male raised and located in the middle class of New England, of French Canadian and northern European ancestry (predominantly German and British), early forties in age, and an evangelical centrist (I'm slightly theologically Reformed with a strong Anabaptist-Wesleyan-Holiness thrust). I'm trusting, though, that this book's theological reflections and practical tools will be enough to help you embrace and embody your calling as reconcilers whatever your place. Consequently, at the end of the chapters there is a section comprised of "Questions for Reflection" and "Practical Next Steps." I urge you to make use of these exercises as I believe they will help stimulate fresh thinking and new actions. Lord knows our world needs that now more than ever—and you can make a difference! So let's get started.

Questions for Reflection

1. How have you experienced difference in your life, e.g., a friendship where there was a contrast in class or ethnicity?

2. Have you ever faced prejudice, injustice, or a bully? How did you handle the situation? What did you learn?

3. Which of the three parts of the reconciling bridge are you most intrigued by and why? Which part do you feel most uncertain or unknowledgeable about and why?

Practical Next Steps

1. If you have never done so, write out part of your story that describes an experience with difference or injustice.

2. Start composing a sketch that conveys aspects of your identity: what is your ancestry? Ethnic background? Education? Religious or faith tradition? The kind of place you were born and raised: a city, suburb, town, or rural area?

1 Your Place

SINCE 2007, I HAVE resided in a particular place: the small, seaside city of Newport, Rhode Island, located at forty-one degrees north latitude and seventy-one degrees west longitude.[1] My adopted home sits on the southern end of Aquidneck Island and is surrounded by the breathtaking beauty of Narragansett Bay. Before I became a resident of Newport, my wife and I only knew the city as tourists, first visiting in July 1998. We have fond memories of strolling on the boardwalk next to sun-kissed Easton's Beach, riding the iconic carousel there, and sauntering down lower Thames Street, browsing through coastal-themed shops selling antiques, shot glasses, paintings, jewelry, and other assorted knickknacks.

Newport is known for its rich history and prestige: the city dates back to 1639 and projects a glamorous image due to its Gilded Age mansions, formerly owned by "American royalty" such as the Vanderbilt family.[2] In 1953, Jacqueline Bouvier married Senator John F. Kennedy downtown at St. Mary's Church; the reception took place at the elegant Hammersmith Farm estate in southern Newport. More recently, billionaire businessman Larry Ellison and comedian Jay Leno both purchased mansions in Newport (Beechwood and Seafair, respectively). Newport, past and present, has been a hot spot for the rich and famous.

However, upon becoming a resident of Newport, I began to see this city was more complicated than advertised. While its prestige is well-earned, Newport also endures high levels of poverty, unemployment, and drug and alcohol addiction, as well as a housing shortage for the impoverished and homeless.[3] Furthermore, upon meeting the director of a local community

1. Okay, *technically* I reside in Middletown, but the Newport city line is only fifteen feet from my house, and I've spent a lot of time in Newport proper.

2. Davis, "Class and Leisure"; Preservation Society of Newport County, "Our Mission."

3. For more info, go to Rhode Island KIDS COUNT's "Factbook Indicators" page, http://www.rikidscount.org/IssueAreas/FactbookIndicators.aspx.

center, I learned that Newport is polarized between the rich and the poor, between millionaires that spend the summer vacationing in the city and many others who subsist on government support.[4] Perhaps most tragically of all, one agency has calculated that Newport has the third highest rate of child abuse and neglect in Rhode Island.[5]

That is a mere snapshot of the place I inhabit. What do you know about the place you call home? Very likely it is more multifaceted than you are currently aware. So because we cannot serve our communities well if our understanding of them is superficial, let's take the opportunity to define the whole idea of *place* more fully.

Defining "place"

Let's imagine that each place is like a diamond. Every diamond has facets: "A facet is a flat surface on the geometric shape of the diamond. . . . The facets are arranged in such a way as to make sure the right amount of light enters the diamond, as well as reflect from the diamond."[6] Now, let's envision that each place has four facets: the concrete, interactive, sacramental, and eschatological. When taken together, these facets, or characteristics, give us a comprehensive picture of place.

The concrete dimension refers to the tangible, created order. The Bible begins with the phrase, "In the beginning God created the heavens and the earth" (Gen 1:1). God fashioned constellations, planets, and black holes in the firmament above, while on our planet he provided rivers, oceans, mountains, trees, grass, etc. Place, then, is materialistic, sensory, and tactile; it is the "physical context of our lives."[7] One can measure the temperature of water and feel its refreshing coolness as it slides down the throat. I can observe the dry texture of sand or the muckiness of mud as my feet press into these surfaces. Every place has an altitude, a scent, a specific collection of flora and fauna, a measurable population of humans and animal

---

4. The director of the Martin Luther King Jr. Center told me the statistics indicated Newport was 40 percent upper class, 20 percent middle class, and 40 percent lower class. I was stunned.

5. Flynn, "Kids Count Eyes Poverty."

6. Cape Town Diamond Museum, "Does a Diamond with More Facets Sparkle More?"

7. Leong, *Race and Place*, 24.

life, a certain kind of built environment located at a specific longitude and latitude. Place is external and quantifiable to us (humans).

Accordingly, place expresses "particularity," a sort of local uniqueness.[8] Consider theologian John Inge's differentiation between *space* and *place*:

> When we think of space, most of us will tend to think of "outer space" and "infinity," but when we think of place, on the other hand, we will tend to think of locality, a particular spot. What is undifferentiated space becomes for us significant place by virtue of our familiarity with it. The two terms might be thought of as tending towards opposite ends of a spectrum which has the local at one end and the infinite at the other. Spaces are what are filled with places.[9]

"Particularity" then, refers to the distinctive elements between various places or localities. That is, every city, town, community, neighborhood, block, park, or domicile presents "'[T]hisness' or *haecceitas* ... [it] is utterly specific and is to be found only in this and that particular."[10] Each place has a specificity to it that sets it apart from other places—concrete and measurable characteristics.

Theologically speaking, particularity finds its pinnacle in the Incarnation[11] of the Son of God, in "Jesus Christ of Nazareth" (Acts 3:5). Professor Stephen Bevans notes,

> God became *flesh* (Jn 1:14), and not generally, but particularly. God became flesh, a human being, in the person of Jesus, a Jew, son of Mary, a male. God became flesh in a human person of such and such a height, with a particular color hair, with particular personality traits, etc.[12]

The Incarnation reveals the value God places on the concrete and difference. The triune God, one being existing in three, distinct persons, has embedded diversity and nuance inside creation, and furthermore, revealed himself through a specific and complex human person entering and occupying

8. Sheldrake, *The Spiritual City*, 123.

9. Inge, *Christian Theology of Place*, 1–2.

10. Sheldrake, *The Spiritual City*, 125. Sheldrake draws from the theology of John Duns Scotus.

11. I am choosing to capitalize 'Incarnation' to emphasize its importance as a theological construct.

12. Bevans, *Models of Contextual Theology*, 12.

an exact location at a certain time in history. The Trinity and Incarnation will be explored further in chapter 2.

In recent decades, particularity has taken on renewed emphasis in response to the international forces of urbanization and globalization, which have wrought social, economic, and technological upheaval and dislocation. Social scientists, philosophers, and geographers detail an attending and pervasive sense of transience and rootlessness. Elie Wiesel labeled the last century the "age of the expatriate, the refugee, the stateless—and the wanderer."[13] There is a sentiment among philosophers and social scientists that the meaning and value of place have been "devalued" or "lost" since the onset of modernity.[14] Sheldrake maintains this mood is especially acute in the West:

> Since the Second World War, people living in cities in Western countries have, in many ways, lost their sense of place identity, because urban existence has increasingly been driven largely by economic rather than communitarian considerations. Thus, the importance of a sense of "place" embedded in a "locality," or "neighborhood" has been de-emphasized for the sake of values such as mobility, centralization, or economic rationalization.[15]

In a world where political, technological, and capitalist entities seek to "McDonaldize" humans through "efficiency, calculability, predictability and control,"[16] a renewed pride of place has ascended. In reaction to this pervasive sense of displacement, people are actively returning to the significance of all things local. One striking illustration is the explosion of craft breweries and brewery jobs. According to journalist Derek Thompson, "a 200-year-old industry has sextupled its establishments and more than doubled its workforce in less than a decade [2008–16]. Even more incredibly, this has happened during a time when U.S. beer consumption declined."[17] Furthermore, Thompson notes this trend occurred in the face of the Anheuser-Busch InBev and MillerCoors duopoly, which has

13. Cited in Inge, *Christian Theology of Place*, 15. Inge includes Edward Casey, Anne Buttimer, Gaston Bachelard, Henri LeFebvre, David Harvey, and Edward Soja in this cohort.

14. Inge, *Christian Theology of Place*, 24–26.

15. Sheldrake, *The Spiritual City,* 118. Also see Gorringe, *Theology of the Built Environment*, 72–76.

16. Ritzger, *The McDonaldization of Society*, 13–15.

17. Thompson, "Craft Beer."

"controlled nearly 90 percent of beer production."[18] The chief economist at the Brewers Association, Bart Watson, gives this explanation: "We've seen three main markers in the rise of craft beer—fuller flavor, greater variety, and more intense support for local businesses."[19] I experienced this trend firsthand when I attempted to purchase a Christmas tree with my younger son, Kelan. On a cold Friday in November we drove to a tree farm in Exeter, Rhode Island. We arrived at the entrance at 3:50 PM and were astonished at the sight of cars backed up at least half a mile on the dirt driveway. My son and I waited twenty minutes for the line to move. At the moment I planned to turn around and head home—in a self-righteous huff—the queue relented. As our car approached the farm, we observed one hundred thirsty fanatics keeping vigil outside, shivering and waiting for Tilted Barn Brewery—the self-proclaimed only barn brewery in Rhode Island—to open its doors at 5 PM and serve its award-winning locally sourced libations. I almost didn't buy a Christmas tree because their intense devotion to socialize and drink beer in a cool, renovated sixty-year-old family-owned barn blocked my access!

Another sign of consumers seeking goods that express their community or city's unique identity is Mapisart.com, my friend Trip Wolfskehl's business. Mapisart is thriving because, apparently, loads of customers want to take vintage maps of their hometowns or favorite vacation spots and have them imprinted on lampshades, throw blankets, skirts, ties, etc. People want to proudly display their most cherished locations (and memories) on their bodies in the form of maps.[20]

To summarize, the concrete aspect helps us to understand that each place has objective traits that make it unique. Those traits are measurable or observable through the five senses. As we live in a world where fewer and

---

18. Thompson, "Craft Beer." Moreover, Thompson notes that while craft breweries are growing exponentially, the "best-selling beers" of the "five major brewers" declined 14 percent.

19. Thompson, "Craft Beer."

20. For the record I am not a paid spokesman for Mapisart.com, although I have a great appreciation for the products. Trip told me his company is consciously rebelling against the "United States of Generica." He touts his recent attendance at the fourth biennial "Power of Place Summit" in Providence, Rhode Island. The purpose is to "bring together change agents committed to shaping a stronger, more vibrant and resilient Rhode Island."

fewer things seem permanent, many people are looking to their particular concrete contexts as something to root themselves in.[21]

If the concrete aspect is all about what we can know of a place through our senses, the interactive aspect is about how we as individuals shape that sensory data. Our worldviews, actions, expectations, aspirations, sins, failures, etc. mold how we feel about, and interact with, where we are. Put differently, "Our world is not just *there*; we are involved in its construction."[22]

The interactive dimension reveals a fabric interwoven by threads of identity, community, and participation. A collection of people located in a shared place collaborate and participate in fashioning, reforming, and forming again an identity through their internal and external interactions, such as the ways they relate to one other and their environment. The idea of *participation* describes how these threads interrelate on a macro scale:

> Some recent writing on the psychology of place speaks of "participation" as a key element in being effectively placed. A true "place," as opposed to a mere "location," invites active participation in the environment. "Environment," in the fullest sense, implies a range of relationships both between people and between the natural context and human beings.[23]

Place then is dynamic: it involves the intersecting of locales, humans, buildings, infrastructure, ecosystems, technology, and communication, which interpenetrate to inform and create various identities.[24]

Furthermore, the interactive aspect, when viewed through a theological and sociological lens, includes the notion of "belonging":

> We all want to locate ourselves in a place that feels like "us." . . . Whatever belonging is, it involves belonging *with* and *to* others in a place. This is how communities work: people and places help us to know who we are. It's fundamentally human to desire

21. Sheldrake states, "It is this sense of placelessness that makes the contemporary Western quest for meaning so concerned with roots." Sheldrake, *The Spiritual City*, 120. For some salient illustrations, see Nash, *Social Movements*, 175–234.

22. Bevans, *Models of Contextual Theology*, 4.

23. Sheldrake, *The Spiritual City*, 120.

24. Missiologist Howard Snyder explains participation in a different way, as a triangular, "*biblically revealed, God-intended relationship* between Yahweh, his people, and the land." Snyder, *Small Voice, Big City*, 238. Similarly, John Inge describes a "relational view of place" that includes God, people, and place. See Inge, *Christian Theology of Place*, 46–47.

belonging, to pursue commonality, to want to know others and be known; this is how we make sense of our identities.[25]

Belonging gives communities a sense of grounding by offering a worldview that helps them assign meaning to the stuff of life: birth, death, work, success, victory, poverty, war, defeat, and suffering.

How communities handle history also shapes their sense of place. A pertinent example is the Newport Middle Passage Port Marker Project, established in 2017. This grassroots group, composed of diverse residents of Newport County, is reappraising the city of Newport's storied history by acknowledging the hard truth that "Newport ships carried 106,000 enslaved Africans across the Atlantic."[26] By creating a memorial, they[27] aim to

> commemorate and honor those many thousands lost in the Middle Passage of the slave trade which was centered in Newport from the 17th to early 19th centuries. We will also will honor those who survived the middle passage, thrived and created a broad and deep heritage which still enriches us to this day.[28]

This project expresses numerous aspects of place, including participation, belonging, identity, history, and narrative. In their estimation, Newport has never fully recognized or reflected on its history of slave trading. It could be argued that the city's wealth and prominence are due, in large measure, to this reprehensible industry. Newport, however, wants its identity defined not by a narrative of victimization and grievance but by one of acceptance, resilience, and increasing justice and flourishing for all. This is a difficult tension to navigate. While we cannot change the past, we can confess the sins of our ancestors, resolve not to repeat them, celebrate those who have overcome these injustices, and work together in the present to collectively forge a better future. Hence, the meaning of place is negotiable and elastic: it involves a complex negotiation between faith/religion, land, participation, belonging, and narrative.

The third aspect of place is the sacramental: places aren't just shaped and defined by humans' presence in them, but also, and most importantly, by God's presence in them. Howard Snyder defines sacrament as "a sign and yet more than a sign. It both witnesses to the operation of God's grace

25. Leong, *Race and Place*, 35.

26. Newport Middle Passage Project, http://newportmiddlepassage.org.

27. While I do not serve in an official position, I am currently supporting these efforts.

28. Newport Middle Passage, http://newportmiddlepassage.org.

and, in some way not fully definable, is a channel or means of that grace."[29] And God gifts places with his presence: "*places are the seat of relations and of meeting and activity between God and the world. . . .* [P]*laces are the chosen seat of God's self-revelation.*"[30] There are special places where God manifested his presence in a unique fashion: Bethel, Mount Moriah, Mount Sinai, Jericho, Bethlehem, etc.

I never grasped this until I spent a semester abroad studying in Jerusalem, Israel, during my junior year of college. Our school, Jerusalem University College, sits on the southwest corner of Mount Zion, overlooking the Hinnom Valley, with the famed artist's village perched directly across the valley from us. A running joke at the college was that hell wasn't all that bad—in fact it appeared peaceful, lovely, and verdant![31] Within a day of arriving, a few of my classmates and I traversed the Old City of Jerusalem, and came upon the Western Wall, also known as the Wailing Wall. This is one of the most sacred sites in the world for Christians, Jews, and Muslims. Jews believe (and archaeology appears to verify) that it is the closest accessible remnant of Solomon's temple that abuts the holy of holies. On the Temple Mount sits al-Aqsa Mosque,[32] the third-holiest site for Muslims, where they assert Muhammad was taken into heaven. Because this area is so revered, it is seriously contested and securely guarded. We were required to pass through two metal detectors and accompanying patdowns to enter the Western Wall area. As we did so, the ladies were sent to the right side, and the men to the left—they are not permitted to pray together. A few Orthodox Jews stood sentry, ensuring Gentiles donned a head covering before they could approach the wall. Little paper hats were handed out to those who were not wearing kippahs (yarmulkes) or caps to ensure absolute compliance with the established protocol. As I came up to the wall, men

---

29. Snyder, *Small Voice, Big City*, 295. For Protestants who may be skeptical of the concept of sacrament, Snyder presents four New Testament words that reinforce this idea. See Snyder, *Small Voice, Big City*, 296–301. Moreover, Inge points out that even John Calvin "referred to the natural world as *theatrum gloriae dei*, a theatre in which the glory of God is manifested." Inge, *Christian Theology of Place*, 62.

30. Inge, *Christian Theology of Place*, 68, 86.

31. Let me explain: Hinnom is linguistically connected to the word *gehenna*, which is the "Greek New Testament word for 'Hell' . . . [and] is a transliteration of the Hebrew Old Testament 'Valley of Hinnom.' . . . Gehenna is a term primarily used in the Synoptic Gospels as a symbol of the eschatological judgment to come (Matt 23:33)" (Winters, "Gehenna," in Barry and Wentz, *Lexham Bible Dictionary*). Tragically, according to 2 Chron 28:3 and 33:6, it was also a place where child sacrifice occurred.

32. Also known as al-Haram al-Sharif.

were chanting Scripture in meditative prayer. Amazingly, tiny pieces of paper were stuffed in between stone cracks of the temple. I found out later they were written prayers. Jews, Christians, and others wanted their deepest longings to be as physically close as possible to the place they believe God's pure and awesome presence most fully resides. Coming from the USA, I had never comprehended the absolute sacredness of a particular location or historical landmark. I understood the need to earnestly protect a nuclear power plant or military base or parts of a state capital, but initially, I found the fervor surrounding the Western Wall and Temple Mount complex disorienting because it seemed so excessive and imposing. But for many religious adherents in our world, certain sites or terrains (e.g., the river Ganges in India) carry a religious or transcendent aura.

The sacramental, however, can exist in less famous places. I think of the two hospital rooms my sons Landon and Kelan were born in, at Skyridge Medical Center in Lone Tree, Colorado, and Newport Hospital, Newport, respectively. I felt the presence, power, and majesty of God in those seemingly sterile and mundane rooms. So too are places that have hosted significant events in our lives: graduations, marriage proposals, weddings, birthdays, baptisms, burials, and so on. Places of suffering, success, delight, and grief are small arenas of God's grace and comfort that mark our human journeys through this life. The major issue is whether we see them as such, whether we pause and perceive God's care in our midst, his revelation in our location.

The fourth aspect of place is the eschatological: place is also future oriented. Theologian John Inge states,

> the biblical sacraments of Baptism and the Eucharist speak of new life coming *only through death*, and thus we must be prepared to relinquish our hold on the places of this world, die to them, if they are to be restored to us in transfigured and glorious state. This is the ultimate sense in which we are to understand the biblical tradition, which, as well as stands valuing place, warns us not to become too attached to it and limit God to it.[33]

The places in our world are only penultimate, because Rev 21–22 presents us with the ultimate place, a gloriously new heaven and earth.[34] In the

33. Inge, *Christian Theology of Place*, 138–39.

34. Whenever I refer to heaven, my intent is to convey the new creation. Too many Christians conceptualize heaven in escapist, ethereal, and disembodied ways (e.g., cherubs playing harps). For more information see Wright, *Surprised by Hope*.

Christian tradition, this will be the eternal home of those who loved and served the triune God on earth. Consequently, this final place was created with assiduous detail and loving craftsmanship: "My Father's house has many rooms; if that were not so, would I have told you that I am going there to prepare a place for you? And if I go and prepare a place for you, I will come back and take you to be with me" (John 14:2–3). Consider Jesus's stunning statement: at the end of time and history, "the ultimate biblical promise is of implacement."[35]

While much more will be said about the final creation in the next chapter, the eschatological facet proposes three implications. First, there will be perfect relations. The depictions of heaven in Scripture reveal a place characterized by complete healing, wholeness, and harmony, and thus void of suffering, sin, evil, and death. In the book of Revelation, "place is presented as relational, and we see the consummation of that threefold union of people, place, and God."[36] Simply put, heaven is the ultimate reconciled place, filled with shalom. Because this is our assured destiny, and Jesus implored his followers to pray, "Your kingdom come, your will be done, on earth as it is in heaven" (Matt 6:10), Christ followers are called to foster reconciliation and promote shalom in their homes, neighborhoods, workplaces, churches, cities, and nations even now, in anticipation of the world to come. Chapter 4 aims to cast this vision.

Another implication of the eschatological aspect is adopting an ethic of good stewardship. Pastor Tim Keller maintains,

> Second Peter 3:10–12 and Revelation 21:1 state that the physical elements of this earth will melt and be destroyed by fire, but Romans 8:19–22 speaks about nature being liberated from its bondage to decay and about our bodies being "redeemed." Taking these two sets of texts together leads us to affirm that some of this present life and world survives and is renewed and that some of it is destroyed.[37]

It is unclear what pieces of creation will be obliterated and which will be refined or become "a transfigured version."[38] Nevertheless, the material world has inherent value due to the first creation and because God may renovate it or transform it in the new creation. Knowing this, Christians are to behave as

---

35. Inge, *Christian Theology of Place*, 139.

36. Inge, *Christian Theology of Place*.

37. Keller, *Center Church*, 228.

38. Inge, *Christian Theology of Place*, 141.

motivated and responsible caretakers of God's creation in the here and now while keeping our gaze ever fixed on the eternal horizon.

A third consequence of the eschatological aspect is a posture of hopeful realism toward all places. That is, Christians acknowledge their position between the first and final creations, which calls for

> an eschatology that holds in creative and redemptive tension the already and the not yet; the world of sin and rebellion, and the world God loves; the new age that has already begun and the old that has not yet ended (Manson 1953:370f); justice as well as justification; the gospel of liberation and the gospel of salvation. Christian hope does not spring from despair about the present. We hope because of what we have already experienced. Christian hope is both possession and yearning, repose and activity, arrival and being on the way. Since God's victory is certain, believers can work both patiently and enthusiastically, blending careful planning with urgent obedience (:149), motivated by the patient impatience of the Christian hope.[39]

In this age, Christians remain "foreigners and exiles" (1 Pet 2:11), called to embody holiness and loving service in every place, while enduring the darkest time of night—right before the break of dawn. Hopeful realism challenges God's people to navigate the narrow channel between the banks of cynicism and the shoals of overconfidence. More to the point, your community deserves your best time, attention, and resources now, because eternity looms ahead.

The lens needed to see your place

Having established the four aspects of place, let's turn our attention to proposing a proper lens. Most jewelers use a loupe, which is a small magnifying glass (sometimes called a monocular), to examine a diamond. The loupe magnifies the diamond (on average 10X) so the jeweler can discover any cracks or blemishes in the diamond.[40]

In this case, the loupe needed to observe the facets of your place contains two magnifying lenses. The first lens is urbanization. Almost every place in America is a city (small through large), is near a city, or is influenced by cities. For instance, the city of Los Angeles is world-renowned

---

39. Bosch, *Transforming Mission*, 508.
40. Clark, "10x Loupe for Gemologists."

for producing a significant number of films and TV series/shows, while San Francisco/Silicon Valley resources and develops a large number of the most popular smartphone applications and platforms, including Facebook, Twitter, Instagram, LinkedIn, and YouTube. I've come to realize when I mention the word "city," many people in North America visualize the iconic and imposing skyline of lower Manhattan, New York City. Here is the reality: it is now estimated that "nearly two-thirds of Americans" live in cities,[41] and the percentage is even higher in the Midwest and West.[42] However, I want to approach cities in a broader sense. While every place is not a city, strictly speaking, many places in the United States—including what urban planners label suburbs, exurbs, towns, and villages—demonstrate urban characteristics, such as density and diversity.[43] This trend is global. Scholars and journalists argue the definitive trait of our age "Is the great, and final, shift of human populations out of rural, agricultural life and into cities. We will end this century as a wholly urban species."[44]

That brings us to the second lens inside the loupe: pursuing a balanced perspective regarding each city or place. That is, for Christians to consciously interpret their home or location within a tension between the poles of sin and grace. It will be beneficial then, to offer a brief overview of the two predominant attitudes within Christianity toward urbanization. Theologians have generally expressed two schools of thought regarding the city or place: the "doom laden view" versus the "endorsement view."[45] The most recent and prominent representatives for these positions are Jacques Ellul (negative view) and Timothy Keller (positive view).[46]

Ellul is known for his book, *The Meaning of the City*, which is "widely recognized as one of the most important twentieth century theological reflections on the city."[47] In particular, he often depicts the cosmopolitan

41. Cohen, "Population Trends in Incorporated Places."

42. United States Census Bureau, "U.S. Cities."

43. For more on this see Keller, *Center Church*, 135–45. Further, McIntosh and McMahan contend, "While there is no commonly accepted definition of an urban city, it is generally assumed that cities of twenty-five hundred or more residents, which are not dependent on an agricultural economy, are urban" (McIntosh and McMahan, *Being the Church*, 59).

44. Saunders, *Arrival City*, 1. Also see Khanna, "Beyond City Limits," and Sassen, "Beyond State-to-State Geopolitics," in A. T. Kearney, *2012 Global Cities Index*, 8.

45. Gorringe, *Theology of the Built Environment*, 140–42.

46. For more information, see Hoffman, "Polar Views of the City," 12–15, 30–31.

47. Toly, "In the City We Trust," 231.

setting using negative language and imagery. For instance, he describes its "judgment," "condemnation," and "curse": "The city is a cursed place—by its origin, its structure, its selfish withdrawal, and its search for other gods."[48] For Ellul, the urban place is "the very center of the world's disorder."[49] This means cities can be destructive:

> Like a vampire, it preys on the true living creation, alive in its connection with the Creator. The city is dead, made of dead things for dead people. . . . We can repeat too often that the city is an enormous man-eater. She does not renew herself from within, but by a constant supply of fresh blood from outside. . . . The city, then, cannot function except as a parasite; it needs constant contributions from the outside.[50]

According to this assessment, cities are not life generating, culture developing, or reconciliation promoting. Rather, they serve as places of rebellion and oppression that dispense chaos and disintegration.

I sympathize with Ellul's judgment. I was raised in rural and suburban places in Vermont and Maine, where it seemed fir trees and squirrels outnumbered humans. As a third grader, I spent countless hours constructing forts out of broken branches behind my apartment. Consequently, it was a shock when I left North America for the first time and traveled to Kolkata (formerly Calcutta), India, during a short-term missions trip my sophomore year of college. Kolkata is considered a megacity and one of the most populous and dense in the world.[51] I scribbled these first impressions in my journal:

> Calcutta assaults the senses. It is loud, noisy, obnoxious, dingy, smelly, dank, crowded, suffocating, obtrusive, etc. The people are friendly and often offer smiles. This place is unlike any other on God's green earth. I feel overwhelmed with excitement and paralyzed with fear. My survival is no longer in my own hands—I am way far out of my element and comfort zone. I am a minority in my religion and color and economic status. It is 6 AM in the morning and yet the city already rages with life . . .

I remember disembarking from a bus in Kolkata and feeling besieged by havoc: cows wandering in the streets, apparently half-dead and destitute

48. Ellul, *Meaning of the City*, 60.
49. Ellul, *Meaning of the City*, 119.
50. Ellul, *Meaning of the City*, 150–51.
51. Allianz, "Top 20 megacities."

people lying in gutters with sewage flowing around them, and children running up to us and begging for money. A while later, our team learned (from Hindus we spoke to) the city was named after the Hindu goddess Kali, the goddess of death/destruction.[52] In some glaring ways, the ethos of the city seemed to reflect its patron god. Nevertheless, our group also encountered many hospitable and generous Indians, discovered delicious cuisine, and became aware of some of the city's fascinating historical and cultural sites. Although these experiences piqued my interest and gave me a desire to further explore Kolkata, part of me was glad once we departed this intense place by boarding a train to Chennai (Madras).[53]

On the other hand is Keller's optimistic position toward cities. He asserts "The city is an intrinsically positive social form with a checkered past and a beautiful future."[54] In Keller's opinion, God "is a city architect, an urban planner, and we are citizens of that city [new Jerusalem]. . . . God invented the city, so we should be for the city."[55] Furthermore, while he maintains the Old Testament presents a dour view of urban places, he points out that the narrative trajectory of the Bible arcs toward the sublime: "As redemptive history progresses, the Bible moves from a largely negative view of the city (emphasizing the city's rebellion) to a more positive one (emphasizing the city's strengths, power, and strategic importance)."[56] Although the history of the city starts with Enoch and progresses to the Tower of Babel on the plain of Shinar (Gen 4:17; 11:1–9), it concludes with the new Jerusalem, a resplendent garden city.

The fact is cities have played a crucial role in the development of human civilization. Historian Joel Kotkin describes three "critical functions" of cities: "the creation of sacred space, the provision of basic security, and the host for a commercial market."[57] We find an illustration in Num 35, which relates how God instructed Moses to institute six "cities of refuge" so that, in the case of accidental manslaughter, the accused would be offered protection and due process as a buffer against an avenger enacting vigilante justice.

52. Cartwright, "Kali."

53. Urban minister Robert Linthicum had a similarly disorienting experience in Kolkata. For his description, see Linthicum, *City of God, City of Satan*, 64–65.

54. Keller, *Center Church*, 151.

55. Keller, *Why God Made Cities*.

56. Keller, *Center Church*, 138. Sheldrake appears to offer a similar interpretation. See Sheldrake, *The Spiritual City*, 15–18. For his part, Gorringe observes "the gloomy assessment of cities in the book of Genesis." Gorringe, *Theology of the Built Environment*, 140.

57. Kotkin, *The City*, xvi.

These designated places were to restrain retaliation (and the accompanying downward spiral of violence) and provide a fair and proper trial. This tradition carries into the present, where certain cities host entities that foster diplomacy, peace, and justice. For instance, the United Nations General Assembly is located in New York City, and The Hague, Netherlands, is home to the International Criminal Court. Some localities possess the financial resources, infrastructure, legal and educational support, etc. to serve the cause of righteousness with more effectiveness than others.

In addition to providing justice, cities can oftentimes act as centers of vitality, including lucrative job prospects, scientific and technological development, and artistic creativity. Economist Edward Glaeser notes cities "have been engines of innovation since Plato and Socrates bickered in an Athenian marketplace."[58] Further, many cities provide a wide variety of jobs and thus "prosperity," defined as "per capita output and income."[59] Because a high percentage of people in these places have occupations that contribute social, cultural, and economic capital, they have higher rates of happiness: "Across countries, reported life satisfaction rises with the share of the population that lives in cities, even when controlling for the countries' income and education."[60] Urban places can offer many opportunities for humans to flourish in their lives and vocations.

Ultimately then, every city and place demonstrates positive and negative characteristics, containing elements of both sin and grace. Consequently, it is best if you view your city or place within the following tension:

> The city is both Babylon, the place of alienation, exile, estrangement and violence, and Jerusalem, the place where God dwells, sets God's sign, and invites humankind to peace. This twofold imaging of the city calls for a dialectic. Any city is always at any one time both Babylon and Jerusalem, as we are reminded by Jesus's description of Jerusalem, the city of peace, as the one who stones the prophets (Luke 19.41).[61]

Your place, like civilization as a whole, is both broken and beautiful. It is both Babylon and Jerusalem: marked by change and stability, death and flourishing, violence and justice, oppression and opportunity. This means Christians are called to avoid the extremes of despair on one end, and idealization on

58. Glaeser, *Triumph of the City*, 1.
59. Glaeser, *Triumph of the City*, 7.
60. Glaeser, *Triumph of the City*, 7–8.
61. Gorringe, *Theology of the Built Environment*, 140.

the other. Despair may make you blind to the ways cities offer forms of justice and opportunity; idealization may cause you to readily overlook the fractures and failures of your place.

I cycled through both of these extremes in my former views of Newport. When I was just a tourist there, Newport's elegant architecture, proud history, sumptuous cuisine, quaint boutiques, and lovely beaches captivated my imagination. Newport had a clear identity: "the city by the sea." However, upon becoming a resident, I then experienced a season of disillusionment. It seemed Newport was a haven for the rich, powerful, and famous, leaving the rest of us to scrape together a sparse existence, especially the poor, minority groups, and immigrants. My home is transient due to the constant influx and outflux of tourists, service industry workers, yacht/boating enthusiasts, and military members briefly stationed at the local Navy base, Naval Station Newport. I grew annoyed by the bitterly chilly winters, poor roads, and high cost of living.

It took a while for my perspective to mature, for me to comprehend and appreciate the complexity of my place, interspersed by layers of grace and sin. My vision is now becoming more rounded and nuanced. I am aware of the non-profit organizations doing significant work with those wrestling with poverty, especially children and teens. I am also participating in and providing leadership for an emerging spiritual revitalization of Newport County and Rhode Island, including united prayer and supporting local nonprofits— more on this later. Nevertheless, I recognize my knowledge is incomplete; I am still learning, my journey continues. I suggest the same applies to you. If you want to develop a well-rounded understanding of your place, embrace the lens of tension. When peering at your place, aim your sight between the poles of sin and grace—of Babylon and Jerusalem.

If you are truly committed, then sit down and start to sketch out a profile of your place using the four aspects described earlier: the concrete, interactive, sacramental, and eschatological. This summary could include statistics, stories, and personal reflections. Specifically, what are the longitude and latitude? How is it organized from a civic perspective: a city, town, suburb, exurb, unincorporated, or rural area? What is the population, racial and ethnic composition, age, and average income?[62] What are the elevation, climate, major geographical features, etc.? With respect to the interactive facet, what is your locale's history? What is it famous for? How could it be considered

---

62. Here are multiple ways to obtain this info: go to census.gov or if you have the resources, purchase a Percept report at http://www.perceptgroup.com/.

infamous? In terms of the sacramental dimension, what special or sacred events have occurred in your region or neighborhood: a revival meeting, the dedication of a religious building like a church/synagogue/mosque, protest, march, historic vote (e.g., the civil rights march across Edmund Pettus Bridge in Selma, Alabama, in 1963)? It might include a tragedy that brought the community together, like a terrorist attack or devastating fire. Lastly, in what ways does your place reflect glints of heaven: gestures or communities of kindness, righteousness, justice, healing, and so on?

Now, which parts of this profile reflect brokenness and evil? Which parts shine the loveliness of God's kingdom? If you are not sure, do some interviews. Canvass business owners, civic and nonprofit leaders, clergy, and educators. Ask what the problems are, what is failing and broken. On the other hand, what are the strengths and opportunities of your place? Inquire who wields the power and who is weak, marginalized, even invisible. Go to a part of town you've never been to, or driven through, and spend thirty minutes walking the streets, slowly, smelling, listening, in a prayerful posture.

When I first moved to Newport, I spent hours meandering around an area two miles northwest of our church, which is predominantly government-subsidized housing. I wanted to sense the sights, smells, sounds, the spiritual atmosphere, the vibe. Were people friendly and engaging? Hostile? Apathetic or distracted? The stereotype of the space surrounding Miantonomi Park was racist: dirty, flashy cars, crime ridden, drug infested, low employment and income, no ambition, uneducated, populated by minorities, mostly blacks and Latinos. With the benefit of more time and greater investigation, I have peered past this typecasting to see a spectrum of dysfunctional to wonderful people inhabiting complex lives, but it started by ambling around with my senses fully attuned.[63]

The crux to comprehending you place is to forgo caricature. It involves exploring your community with a curious mind and open heart. It also means embracing a tension between Babylon and Jerusalem, between brokenness and beauty. Your place is dynamic—simultaneously decaying and flourishing.

With this perspective in mind, we turn our gaze to three categories that influence how we perceive our homes and neighborhoods and thus shape our reconciling commission.

---

63. Since that time, a number of friends and ministry colleagues have moved into that neighborhood and our church has engaged in many outreach events and initiatives, giving me a more multifaceted comprehension of this Newport neighborhood.

The Gal 3:28 triad

Galatians 3:26–28 is a classic text on Christian identity. In it, the Apostle Paul states,

> So in Christ Jesus you are all children of God through faith, for all of you who were baptized into Christ have clothed yourselves with Christ. There is neither Jew nor Gentile, neither slave nor free, nor is there male and female, for you are all one in Christ Jesus.

In the process of refuting Jewish Christians known as "Judaizers," who insisted Gentile Christians be circumcised to be truly saved, Paul indicates baptism into Christ (regeneration) resets human identity. Specifically, "Our primary identity as Christians is as 'Children of God.' . . . The gospel transcends the importance of other, lesser identities."[64] Indeed, being an adopted child of our heavenly Father, or as Jesus called him *Abba* (Aramaic for "daddy") surpasses the now secondary identities of ethnicity,[65] class, and sex.[66]

So why does Paul cite these three categories in particular? I would argue that they're examples of significant division in the world and the Church, both in the ancient world and at present. Theologian Michelle Lee-Barnewall asserts they "represented some of the leading ways people were separated from one another and the sources of the most bitter hostility and animosities."[67] Indeed, this triad expresses deep identities embedded within humanity, yet infected by sin and poisoned by evil forces:

---

64. Kim, Matthew D. and Scott M. Gibson, eds. *The Big Idea Companion for Preaching and Teaching: A Guide from Genesis to Revelation.*

65. I prefer the term "ethnicity" to "race." There is one human race composed of many ethnic groups (*ethnos* in Koine Greek—e.g., Matt 28:19 and Rev 7:9). McIntosh and McMahan state, "Technically, the word *race* is not a biblical term. . . . Even secular writers and researchers now understand the concept of race to be nothing more than a social construction. . . . [S]cientists generally group all of humanity into forty-two native population groups that form nine population clusters. . . . *Multi-ethnic* reflects more accurately the biblical concept of 'the peoples'" (*Being the Church*, 23–25).

66. Scholar Ronald Fung observes, "It is noteworthy that in the third antithesis the words used are not the customary terms for man and woman but the more technical terms denoting male and female, thus indicating that what is in view is the general relationship between the sexes" (Fung, *Epistle to the Galatians*, 175). Thus I agree with Fung that Paul is addressing sex rather than gender in this text. Some scholars appear to conflate sex and gender when commenting on this text. For example, see Keller, *Galatians for You*, 92–93.

67. Lee-Barnewall, *Neither Complementarian nor Egalitarian*, 87–88.

> The three pairs of opposites Paul listed stand for the fundamental cleavages of human existence: ethnicity, economic capacity, and sexuality. Race, money, and sex are primal powers in human life. No one of them is inherently evil; rather they are the stuff of which life itself is made. . . . Yet each of these spheres of human creativity has become degraded and soiled through the perversity of sin. . . . Indeed, outside of Christ the primal forces represented by these three polarities are controlled and manipulated by the elemental spirits of the universe (*stoicheia tou kosmou*; Gal 4:3, 9).[68]

So while God created racial and ethnic variety,[69] economic and vocational differences, and male and femaleness, sin and the "powers and authorities" (Col 2:15) of this dark world take difference and turn it into division marked by separation, alienation, and domination (power plays). Unsurprisingly, we can see plenty of examples of these divisions all around us.

Regarding racial/ethnic divides, "in the United States, one of the largest urban issues has been racism and the need for reconciliation."[70] I know this because of my relationship with my good friend (and ministry partner) Steve Robinson. Steve founded and leads Crosspoint Church, a multiethnic church in Newport, Rhode Island. Steve has bravely shared with me the stories of what it's like being a black man in America. For him and the community he leads, there are stories of profiling, bullying, and discrimination. But he's not alone. Another good friend of mine is Korean American. His family, including three young sons, have heard racial slurs and experienced other forms of ignorance and abuse that make me resonate with his anger and grief. I hope you agree with me our land needs racial and ethnic healing.

Unfortunately, numerous signs indicate racism and prejudice also operate on a systemic level. One example sociologists point to is the US criminal justice system. Black people, especially males, are disproportionately convicted, incarcerated, and put to death. Scholars and activists such as

---

68. George, *Galatians*, 284–85.

69. Brenda Salter McNeil maintains the cultural mandate of Gen 1:28 reveals God's desire for diversity: "the result of God's command to fill the earth would be *difference*" (Salter McNeil, *Roadmap to Reconciliation*, 24). Further, Rev 7:9 indicates heaven is multiethnic.

70. Sunquist, *Understanding Christian Mission*, 360. Michael Wear, who worked closely with President Obama, concurs: "In the coming years, two political and cultural issues will deeply affect how Christians act and are perceived in our nation. The first is the area of racial justice and reconciliation. Racial inequalities and injustices have become a greater part of our public discussion and politics" (Wear, *Reclaiming Hope*, 216–17).

Michelle Alexander[71] and Bryan Stevenson[72] attribute these statistics to the ways discrimination influences some cities' or state's approaches to policing, prosecuting, and sentencing of criminals, along with federal or state support for the prison-industrial complex. This reality is troubling and will arouse genuine concern and conviction for followers of Jesus.

Yet tragically, more often than not, it appears many Christians have perpetuated this sin rather than fostered healing and reconciliation. Christians in America have often enabled racism in many guises, from slavery to Jim Crow laws. A number of seminal books, including *Divided by Faith*,[73] *The Color of Compromise*,[74] and *The Christian Imagination*[75] rightly accuse the Church of a long history of "complicity" when it comes to systemic prejudice. This has led numerous Christians to call the Church to lead in the area of reparations, which appears to align with the Old Testament prophetic call for justice and righteousness, including financial restitution for one's sins.[76]

The second divide pertains to class, which intersects with race. I am suggesting that slavery ("slave nor free") is comparable to class. In the ancient world, slavery, like class today, was an economic and cultural construct that dictated social stratification.[77] By and large, class is shaped by privilege, immigration or citizenship status, wealth, poverty, geography, education, socialization, and cultural factors. Expert Ruby Payne demonstrates that class comprises more than simple economics: it is also influenced by norms, "hidden rules," language ("discourse patterns"), education, and relationships (social networks).[78] Class acts as an identity marker or value system that deeply affects how people perceive themselves and view others. It is both invisible and visible.[79]

---

71. Alexander, *New Jim Crow*.

72. Stevenson, *Just Mercy*.

73. Emerson and Smith, *Divided by Faith*.

74. Tisby, *Color of Compromise*.

75. Jennings, *Christian Imagination*.

76. Kwon and Lyons, "Race Reparations." Ta-Nehisi Coates, who is not a Christian, makes a persuasive case for reparations in chapter 7 of his book *We Were Eight Years in Power*.

77. For more information on slavery in the ancient world, see Ruprecht, "Slave, Slavery," in Hawthorne et al., *Dictionary of Paul*, 881–83.

78. Payne, *Framework for Understanding Poverty*, 2–3.

79. For narrative accounts regarding the challenges of "class passing" see Vance, *Hillbilly Elegy*, and Mahdawi, "'Class-passing.'"

Two observations about class are relevant here. Income inequality is growing, revealing greater disparities between the rich and the poor. For example, college graduates make more money over the course of their lives, have better health, and live longer than less educated people.[80] Oxfam International asserts, "Eight men now control as much wealth as the world's poorest 3.6 billion people. . . . Such dramatic inequality is trapping millions in poverty, fracturing our societies, and poisoning our politics."[81] Christians who occupy the middle or upper classes (or those who've had little contact with financial hardship) will do their best to educate themselves in the areas of class, poverty alleviation, and economic justice. Tim Keller frames it this way:

> Job says he *wears* [cf Job 29:14] justice, suggesting that it is always on his mind, he is always looking for ways to do it. Psalms 41:1 says, "Blessed is the man who considers the poor," and the Hebrew word translated as "considers" means to give sustained attention to a subject and then to act wisely and successfully with regard to it. God does not want us to merely give the poor perfunctory help, but to ponder long and hard about how to improve their entire situation.[82]

Helpfully Keller presents three levels of support Christians can offer: "*relief, development,* and *social reform*."[83] The first level is meeting critical needs like food and shelter; the second involves empowering individuals and groups toward greater self-reliance; the third level (social reform) addresses unjust laws and social structures that entrap people.[84] When Christians consider engaging in at least one of these levels, it may help foster more flourishing while combating inequality. The key is to move toward aligning ourselves with God's vision for shalom (i.e., Amos 5, Mic 6) by promoting opportunity and stability in American society. On the other hand, one need look no further than the bloody French Revolution of the late 1700s to grasp the potential for violence that class conflict can precipitate if unresolved.

---

80. "College Graduates live longer"; Cook, "Seriously, Go to College."

81. Kottasova, "These 8 Men."

82. Keller, *Generous Justice*, 110. I highly recommend this book as a primer on economic justice from a biblical perspective.

83. Keller, *Generous Justice*, 113.

84. Keller, *Generous Justice*, 115–34.

Second, economists are pointing out the numerous ways race and class are inextricably intertwined. For instance, Thomas Shapiro claims, "it is crucial to understand that the trends toward greater income and wealth inequality are converging with a widening racial wealth gap. The typical African American family today has less than a dime of wealth for every dollar of wealth owned by a typical white family."[85] Additionally, Nobel laureate Joseph Stiglitz observes that in spite of major legislative victories (e.g., the Fair Housing Act), "there has been no significant closing of the gap between the income of African-Americans (or Hispanics) and white Americans the last 30 years."[86] America's history of racism continues to have negative repercussions for minorities attempting to rise within our class structure.[87]

The third polarity listed in Gal 3:28 is sex. Scholars observe that in the original language Gal 3:28 states "male and female," likely a reference to Gen 1:27. This reinforces the interpretation the Apostle Paul is referring to sex rather than gender. To clarify, I agree with theologian Megan DeFranza's definitions: "sex difference is rooted in the body—chromosomes, hormone levels, internal and external reproductive organs . . . gender is influenced by physiology but is lived (some say performed) according to cultural patterns."[88] In the Christian worldview, one's sex is not his or her most defining characteristic because all people are worthy of respect and dignity as humans made in the image of God. Furthermore, according to Jesus, sexuality will not have the same prominence or identity-forming power in heaven as it does on earth: "At the resurrection people will neither marry nor be given in marriage; they will be like the angels in heaven."[89]

85. Shapiro, *Toxic Inequality*, 15.

86. Stiglitz, *Great Divide*, 140–41.

87. For a devastating analysis, see the chapter "The Case for Reparations" in Coates, *We Were Eight Years in Power*, 163–208.

88. DeFranza, *Sex Difference in Christian Theology*, xiv. She then differentiates between "transsexuals—persons who feel a sense of disjunction between their bodily sex and their gender identity—and intersex—persons whose bodies do not line up clearly with the medical norms for biological maleness or femaleness."

89. Matt 22:30. Scholar Timothy George comments this "is at least one hint in the New Testament that the distinction of gender is intended for this temporal life only and will not be reconstituted at the resurrection" (George, *Galatians*, 290).

Serious inequalities between males and females, however, continue to plague the United States. This is seen by the #MeToo[90] and Time's Up[91] movements, which are confronting the prevalence of sexual harassment and assault, and the widespread pay gap between males and females, especially in the technology[92] and entertainment industries.[93] Worst of all, one in three women in the US have "experienced some form of contact sexual violence in their lifetime" and "91% of victims of rape and sexual assault are female."[94] According to the United Nations Office on Drugs and Crime, 71 percent of human trafficking victims are women and girls.[95] These statistics are unacceptable, for God loves and values women just as much as men.

The role social media and partisan politics play in turning differences into divisions

Bridging ethnic, class, and sex differences is difficult in and of itself; yet the challenge is further exacerbated by the rising tide of social media and rancorous partisan politics in American society. There is a way in which these entities stoke existing tensions, fueling them so as to turn God-given difference (e.g., ethnicity and sex) into bitter division and alienation. Although there are positive ways social media can foster reconciling by helping people rally around a cause, the purpose here is to highlight the disadvantages of our digitally driven, internet-focused society.

We all know that social media—especially platforms like Facebook, Instagram, Twitter, Snapchat, LinkedIn, and Tik Tok—are wildly popular. But popular does not necessarily translate to beneficial. We must seriously consider the negative effects of social media and the ways it hinders incarnational ministry if we are to answer the call to be Christ's reconcilers in our divided places on earth. While I am not advocating Christians abandon social media altogether, I am pressing for a more reflective and strategic engagement. More pointedly, due to the West's obsession with social media, I want to offer an overcorrection by presenting five

90. "Me Too," https://metoomvmt.org/.

91. "Time's Up," https://www.timesupnow.com/.

92. Mundy, "Silicon Valley."

93. Langone, "#MeToo and Time's Up."

94. National Sexual Violence Resource Center, "Statistics."

95. United Nations, "Report."

prominent weaknesses of our online lives. Social media is disembodied, addictive, dehumanizing, tribal, and docetic.

To start, from a theological perspective, a core tenet of the gospel is the wondrous announcement that "the Word became flesh and made his dwelling among us. We have seen his glory, the glory of the one and only Son, who came from the Father, full of grace and truth" (John 1:14). God fully entered the human condition by landing on this dysfunctional third rock from the sun. Think about it: the Son of God was pushed through Mary's birth canal; soiled his diapers; learned to walk, talk, read, and write; and went through puberty (now *that's* love!).

Bono, the lead singer of the band U2, describes the moment he was awakened to the power of the Incarnation. He was returning home to Dublin after a long concert tour. Because it was Christmas Eve, he attended a worship service at the famed St. Patrick's Cathedral in Dublin, an Anglican church built circa 1220. Of course the usher gave him a terrible seat, obstructed by a massive pillar. He was exhausted and trying desperately to keep his eyes open, when he had an astonishing epiphany:

> The idea that God, if there is a force of Logic and Love in the universe, that it would seek to explain itself is amazing enough. That it would seek to explain itself and describe itself by becoming a child born in straw poverty, in [s**t] and straw ... a child ... I just thought: "Wow!" Just the poetry ... Unknowable love, unknowable power, describes itself as the most vulnerable. There it was. I was sitting there, and it's not that it hadn't struck me before, but tears came streaming down my face, and I saw the genius of this, utter genius of picking a particular point in time. ... There must be an incarnation. Love must be made flesh.[96]

The Incarnation of Jesus Christ reveals God's desire to connect with, rescue, and heal our deformed world. This act of tremendous risk and vulnerability shows the lengths God went to touch his image bearers and identify with them by experiencing their pains and joys. Thus, the Incarnation is the highest and purest form of communication. This means, when possible, Christians will prioritize presence, touch, and face-to-face interaction.

On the contrary, a serious flaw of social media is that it is inherently *disembodied* or *unincarnational*. It allows us to detach from live, human contact. At its worst, social media is the absence of authentic and meaningful presence: eye contact, high fives and hugs, detecting voice modulation,

96. Assayas, *Bono*, 139.

reading body language and facial expressions. Why make the effort to meet with you if I can send you a direct message? Or "like" your post? It's easier, quicker, cleaner—and detached.

One consequence of disembodiment is that we can carefully curate what others see and thus how they perceive us. From his perspective as a divorce lawyer, James Sexton—who has been party to over one thousand divorces—labels Facebook an "Infidelity-Generating Machine":

> If you're vaguely unhappy with your relationship or marriage, and especially if you're *more* than vaguely unhappy with it: Stay away from Facebook. The vast majority of what you'll find there is unhappiness masked as happiness. . . . Facebook is the single greatest breeding ground ever for infidelity. . . . I don't keep detailed statistics on these things, but if I had to estimate I would say I get two or three new cases per week that feature infidelity that started or was made easier to perpetuate by Facebook. Who knew one platform could cause so much chaos?[97]

This is precisely why a friend of mine refers to Facebook as "Facade-Book." It is much harder to manipulate our image when communication is embodied—there is no filter in live, present interactions. When face to face, people can discern vocal inflection, body posture, eye movement, etc. In other words, we can more readily and confidently perceive jubilance, tension, rigidity, sarcasm, sly humor, sadness, or ambivalence. So the first weakness of social media is disembodiment, which can enable deception.

Another consequence of disembodiment is it undermines meaningful communication through persistent distraction. Most people engage social media through their smartphones, which are now ubiquitous. Researcher Adrian Ward conducted a study exploring how smartphones influence cognition and thus workplace performance. His experiments concluded smartphones cause "brain drain": "the mere presence of consumers' smartphones can adversely affect two measures of cognitive capacity—available working memory capacity and functional fluid intelligence."[98] Smartphones (with their ongoing status updates) affect a person's ability to focus, listen, process information, problem-solve, and collaborate. Social media is the constant burst of breeze nudging the tightrope walker off his line. Personally, this is a vexing problem for me as a leader: During our church staff meetings, I ask whether anyone is awaiting an important call. If not, we mute our phones

97. Sexton, *If You're in My Office*, 114–15.
98. Ward et al., "Brain Drain," 140–54.

and place them in the middle of the table. Otherwise, some staff members will receive a text, notification, or snap with their phones, read a meme, laugh out loud, and get our agenda sidetracked.

This challenge points to a second major flaw: social media is designed to be *addictive*, and increasingly entraps its users. Sean Parker, the former president of Facebook, confessed the platform invented the "like" button to dispense "a little dopamine hit" to users so they would be behaviorally conditioned to keep returning and uploading more content. He admits, "It's a social validation feedback loop . . . exactly the kind of thing that a hacker like myself would come up with, because you're exploiting a vulnerability in human psychology."[99] Consequently, scientists and researchers are increasingly evaluating the ways social media functions as an addictive drug.[100] This disturbing trend struck me like smelling salts when I took my mother out to lunch for her birthday recently. On a sunny Saturday in June, we drove to an upscale restaurant and were seated on an outdoor patio that offered riveting ocean views. As we were chatting, I noticed a married couple (mid-thirties in age) at an adjacent table. They were both glued to their phones, scrolling through (presumably) pictures, status updates, or a fantasy sports team lineup. Occasionally, the wife looked up and made a remark to her husband. Without bothering to glance up in acknowledgment, he nodded, or gave a one-word answer. They continued this pattern after being served their meal. By the time they departed fifty minutes later, it appeared he had spoken fewer than twenty words. At the time, I was alternately fascinated and jarred by this peculiar scene—one that appears to be increasingly common. I wonder: if we cannot enjoy fine cuisine, delightful conversation, and breathtaking sights, aren't we losing the most primal and authentic pleasures of humanity?

Our cultural addiction is metastasizing. Psychologist Jean M. Twenge documents the rise of "iGen," those born between 1995 and 2012, who matured at the tipping point (2012) where over half the US population owned a smartphone.[101] Indeed, it is estimated that three-fourths of teens own a smartphone.[102] The results of Twenge's two decades of research regarding "generational differences" are stunning: "Rates of teen depression and suicide have skyrocketed since 2011. It's not an exaggeration to describe iGen

---

99. Solon, "Ex–Facebook President Sean Parker."

100. Smith, "Social Media."

101. Twenge, "Have Smartphones Destroyed a Generation?"

102. Twenge, "Have Smartphones Destroyed a Generation?"

as being on the brink of the worst mental-health crisis in decades. Much of this deterioration can be traced to their phones."[103]

The third notable weakness of social media is it can be *dehumanizing*. Many users are unaware the companies that offer apps and platforms are objectifying their customers/clients by commodifying them. We may think we are "using" social media, but social media is really "using" us. We are not consuming social media so much as social media is consuming us, or more specifically, our data—what we like, care about, are interested in. This has led to some justified backlash. In their book *New Power*, computer scientists and activists Jeremy Heimans and Henry Timms assert that social media users are unwittingly joining "participation farms" where tech platforms test new marketing methods and ideas on their human subjects; in addition these companies also gather their user's data, create profiles, and sell that information to other companies or partisan-political organizations, like Cambridge Analytica. What's more, Harvard professor Shoshana Zuboff penned the provocative work, *The Age of Surveillance Capitalism: The Fight for a Human Future at the New Frontier of Power*. Zuboff argues that major corporations like Google and Facebook are seeking to control or "automate" us by observing our behavior and then preying on it, e.g., noticing what time a person browses Amazon at night and then using targeting ads to get him or her to buy a product. Her book labels these practices a new form of totalitarianism. Yikes![104]

The fourth concern I want to highlight is that social media promotes digital tribalism by encouraging participants to cocoon themselves within various silos (e.g., religious, ideological, political, ethnic, class, etc.). Theo Wilson, a black poet, actor, and activist, discovered an alternate world when he created a ghost profile and went undercover inside white supremacist chat rooms. For approximately eight months, he assumed the identity of a racist troll. He quickly learned these silos contained sharply defined microcultures: the participants had their own dialect, repeating identical terms and phrases, unswervingly cited the same historical "facts" and studies to prove the inferiority of blacks, and visited a few select approved websites and YouTube channels for information. Along the way, Wilson came to this realization: "The Internet is sort of what a car is to road rage. The glass and steel create this bubble of perceived safety, which amplifies people's rage, but

---

103. Twenge, "Have Smartphones Destroyed a Generation?"

104. Even if you don't read Zuboff's book, in the very least, read a few good reviews—you won't regret it.

keeps them from having to deal with the consequences of that rage."[105] This is a keen insight. The internet, along with its sibling devices (social media, smartphones, etc.), promotes disembodied communication between God's image-bearing beings with eternal souls. How is our humanity diminished when our communication is reduced to fragmented pieces of data traversing across fiber-optic cables or satellite lines?

This insight reveals one of the more sinister by-products of tribal cocooning: segregation. Through the internet people can quarantine themselves from people who are "different," which in turn makes it easier to generalize and dislike them. In this scenario, the "other" becomes a label, an epithet: "liberal," "conservative," "elitist," "redneck," etc. Theo Wilson agrees: "[Digital devices] reinforce our wants and desires, so if these desires are immature, we never grow. Racism is a comfy cage, and technology hasn't provided the key for getting out. We need to have courageous, face-to-face conversations with difficult people outside of the security of our laptops."[106] As will be explained in chapter 2, this contradicts the relational nature and redemptive plan of the Holy Trinity in which the Father sends his Son to engage alienated sinners, and calls his disciples to do the same. Theologian Miroslav Volf describes this as *embrace*, "the will to give ourselves to others and 'welcome' them, to readjust our identities to make space for them."[107] In these ways, social media can oftentimes undercut the Christian identity and calling to show care for and hospitality to the other.

Segregation and silos bring social disintegration. For this reason, social media's former champions are swiftly becoming its latest detractors. A former vice president at Facebook, Chamath Palihapitiya, declared, "The short-term, dopamine-driven feedback loops that we have created are destroying how society works. No civil discourse, no cooperation, misinformation, mistruth. . . . This is a global problem. It is eroding the core foundations of how people behave."[108]

We arrive at the fifth and final negative consequence. At its darkest, our digital-technological selves carries similarities to the first-century heresy known as Docetism, depicted in 1 John. Docetism was promulgated by false teachers who maintained that Jesus only "appeared" in human

---

105. Theo Wilson cited in Holley, "A Black Man Went Undercover."

106. Theo Wilson cited in Holley, "A Black Man Went Undercover."

107. Volf, *Exclusion and Embrace*, 29.

108. Wong, "Former Facebook executive."

form, like an apparition.[109] They argued this based on the Hellenistic-gnostic notion that the body is evil, while the spirit is pure. According to their logic, if Jesus was sinless, he could not have taken on a human body, as it would have sullied his holy and exalted state as God. They used this heresy to justify promoting sinful behavior. The reasoning goes like this: the body is like a "dirty receptacle" that will be tossed upon death. Your soul is separate from your body and so is undefiled, but upon death will be freed from its bodily prison. In the meantime, you can abuse your body—it won't matter in the long run.

The Apostle John, however, refutes their claims by reaffirming the validity and necessity of the Incarnation. He asserts that he, along with many others, have "heard," "seen," and "touched" the incarnate Son of God (1 John 1:1). Later, he contends, "Every spirit that acknowledges that Jesus Christ has come in the flesh is from God, but every spirit that does not acknowledge Jesus is not from God. This is the spirit of the antichrist" (1 John 4:2–3). First John then, indicates Jesus showed us what it means to be authentically and completely human.

This is instructive for Christians traversing the digital highway. As Marshall McLuhan famously declared, "The medium is the message." Our social media selves tend to be more "docetic" (apparitions) than "incarnate" (flesh that is heard, seen, and touched). Apps and chat rooms can facilitate deception through image management, allowing users to present selected parts of themselves while hiding others. A person can construct a mirage by accentuating, or applying a filter to some pieces while concealing the whole, nuanced person. Ironically, while one may curate his image, other users may be doing the same thing at the same time. This brings profound disfiguration as one apparition appears to another.[110]

What can be done to counteract these five damaging effects? A few recommendations are in order. First, ask yourself why you use social media: Do I have a clear purpose, e.g., to stay in touch with family and friends? My church has many active-duty members of the military who utilize Facebook and Instagram while stationed across the globe to post pictures and videos of their children for friends and family members to enjoy. Or do you use it to veg out, escape boredom, pass the time? The

---

109. For more info see Barker, *Zondervan NIV Study Bible.*

110. When taken to the extreme, this behavior concludes in pain, betrayal, and distrust—just watch the controversial and devastating MTV show *Catfish.*

former use is connectional; the latter is more consumer oriented.[111] Further, make a point of going on social media fasts. Perhaps one day per week. Set limits on your smartphone or iPad.[112] After ninety minutes of usage per day, your phone will shut off access to the app. Consider using only one platform: Facebook or Instagram; LinkedIn or Twitter. The problem is that many people use multiple platforms throughout the day. If you are struggling with social media usage, get an accountability partner or join a support group.[113] I also love the idea proposed by pastor and author John Mark Comer: to establish a "digital rule of life": "1) Digital Detox, 2) Digital Sabbath, 3) Parent your phone, 4) Get a real alarm clock (to get your phone out of your room), 5) No devices in kid's rooms or men's rooms,'6) Turn off all alerts, 7) Don't make TV the locus point of your home, 8) Write up a list of rules."[114]Additionally, consider reading the helpful books *Digital Minimalism: Choosing a Focused Life in a Noisy World* by Cal Newport or *The Tech-Wise Family: Everyday Steps for Putting Technology in its Proper Place* by Andy Crouch.

Moreover, intentionally rephrase the standard terminology so it reflects reality. Our words have the power to affirm, disrupt, or redefine the prevailing status quo. Instead of saying "I have 789 Twitter followers," insert the phrase "Twitter contacts." From a Christian perspective, "follower" must not be reduced so as to mean "elects to receive status updates." Jesus summoned his first disciples, Peter and Andrew, with the phrase "Come, follow me and I will send you out to fish for people" (Matt 4:19). The Christian life is no less than obedient, joyful, and sacrificial pursuit of the suffering God-Man: "Whoever wants to be my disciple must deny themselves and take up their cross daily and follow me" (Luke 9:23). Refuse to use the lingo "Facebook friend" but instead use "Facebook fan" or "Facebook acquaintance." Why? Jesus declared, "Greater love has no one than this: to lay down one's life for one's

---

111. Chamath Palihapitiya challenged an audience at Stanford Business School to "soul search" about how they view and interact with social media, because "your behaviors, you don't realize it, but you are being programmed. . . . It was unintentional, but now you gotta decide how much you're going to give up, how much of your intellectual independence" (Wong, "Former Facebook executive").

112. I recommend looking into the HOLD App, which employs a brilliant points and rewards system: https://www.holdstudent.com/.

113. For more information go to "Time to Log Off," https://www.itstimetologoff.com/. This site is a wealth of information on internet addiction, and includes resources to how to do a "Digital Detox," and other concrete actions.

114. Comer, "Case for a Digital Asceticism."

friends. You are my friends if you do what I command" (John 15:13–14). I'm confident I would sacrifice my life for only a select handful of my Facebook "friends." Let's align our words with God's word so God's reality will invade our sometimes "artificial" (AI) one.

The bottom line is that social media, if used uncritically, can widen our divides. To be faithful reconcilers we must commit to live more reflectively and counterculturally in the digital age.

Partisan politics: tribal gasoline

Few Americans would disagree that partisan politics inflame the tensions in our society. Political scientists contend political polarization, defined as "negatively stereotyp[ing] members of the opposing party" (both Democrats and Republicans), spiked by "50 percent between 1960 and 2010."[115] This is leading to an alarming level of social segregation: Americans that belong to the two major parties are now far less likely than previous generations to socialize with, become friends with, be neighbors with, and even marry their political adversaries.[116] What is the cause for this widening schism? There is a mounting consensus it stems from tribal identity:

> A single vote can now indicate a person's partisan preference *as well as* his or her religion, race, ethnicity, gender, neighborhood, and favorite grocery store. This is no longer a single social identity. Partisanship can now be thought of as a mega-identity, with all the psychological and behavioral magnifications that implies.[117]

The key is that many Americans are now more influenced by partisan identity than ideas or policy positions. Emotionally, psychologically, and relationally, their behavior is shaped by groupthink or herd mentality: "social identity is a deeply embedded psychological orientation toward all social interactions."[118] Consequently, partisans loathe and demonize their opponents. Eminent political scientists Alan Abramowitz and Steven Webster call this phenomenon "negative partisanship," defined as "increasing

---

115. Mason, *Uncivil Agreement*, 3.

116. Mason, *Uncivil Agreement*, 55. Mason estimates "85 percent of the American population" belongs to either of the major parties (4).

117. Mason, *Uncivil Agreement*, 14.

118. Mason, "Ideologues without Issues," 298.

negativism toward the opposing party."[119] This creates a dynamic I call "the fellowship of the negative"—meaning that people define themselves not according to what they are for, but what (or who) they are against. For example, in my pastoral experience, some marriages are not based on mutual love for God, one another, family, Church, and community. Instead, couples bounce from one perceived or fabricated crisis to another where they bond around common enemies or problems. Oftentimes, this is a cloak used to hide their lack of healthy connection. A shared enemy covers the holes beneath. The upshot is this:

> Regardless of the strength of their attachment to the Democratic Party or the Republican Party, American voters in the 21st century are much more likely to hold strongly negative views of the opposing party than in the past. The rise of this sort of negative partisanship in the American electorate has led to the highest rates of party loyalty and straight ticket voting in the past sixty years.[120]

This antipathy provokes an unconscious "sorting": "social identities have repeatedly been found to generate ingroup privilege and outgroup derogation."[121] Consequently, politics is devolving into a zero-sum game that undermines representative democracy: "Group victory is a powerful prize, and American partisans have increasingly seen that goal as more important than the practical matters of governing a nation. . . . Even when there is nothing to fight over, group members want to win."[122] Unfortunately, the end result is "little or no incentive for bipartisan compromise," which leads to "confrontation and gridlock."[123]

Furthermore, a result of political tribalism and negative partisanship is a weakening of the importance, uniqueness, and autonomy of place. As elections become more "nationalized,"[124] party trumps place: party victory takes precedence over local and state matters. Partisan loyalty, in the form of straight ticket voting for the party's presidential contender and Senate and congressional candidates, dominates. Homegrown needs and preferences succumb to the gravitational pull of Washington, DC.

119. Abramowitz and Webster, "All Politics Is National," 15.

120. Abramowitz and Webster, "All Politics Is National," 26.

121. Mason, "Ideologues without Issues," 284.

122. Mason, *Uncivil Agreement*, 4, 11.

123. Abramowitz and Webster, "All Politics Is National," 26.

124. Abramowitz and Webster, "All Politics Is National," 15–26.

This trajectory threatens to corrode our souls, our public discourse, and our communities, institutions, and democracy. There is little flourishing to be had in this toxic environment.

Toxic fusion: a story

I received a whiff of the poisonous potion of social media and tribal politics during the final days of the 2016 presidential campaign. When the infamous *Access Hollywood* recording was released (suspiciously close to voting day for an over decade-old tape) and millions heard the voice of candidate Donald Trump bragging obscenely about forcibly grabbing and kissing women, I lost my cool.[125] My wife warned me to step down, but I was so disturbed as a human being, Christian, and pastor, I posted a link to an article on my Facebook status update with the hashtags #disgusting, #reprehensible, #abhorrent, and #shameful. That was all. I offered no diatribe or commentary. All I wanted to do was express my disapproval of the vile words caught on camera. And to be honest, I didn't feel that was an indication of whom I was voting *for*.

Suddenly my Facebook feed blew up. The first two people to react were women defending Mr. Trump. I was stunned. One was a college friend, and the other a former parishioner who had moved back to Seattle for work. In an accusatory tone they probed, "So you're voting for Hillary Clinton?" I responded: "No, I am only commenting on the content of the recording." The next thing I knew, dozens of people were either attacking Mr. Trump or defending him. The most jarring part of this virtual conflict was that another pastor from Rhode Island, an acquaintance, berated two of my parishioners at length because they were Trump supporters. He had never met them. As expected, they went to great lengths to defend their position. This happened . . . on my feed! After an hour, I commented to my wife, "And they will know we are Christians by our love! How will we all end up in heaven together?" I finally erased the post. Shortly thereafter my pastor friend sent me a direct message apologizing for his behavior and indicating he had done the same to my church members as well.

The incident scared me and scarred me. It demonstrated that partisan politics, when adjudicated over social media, frequently delivers far more

---

125. For the record, although I tend to be a right-leaning centrist, I am registered as *unaffiliated* (some might call it "independent") in Rhode Island and voted for a third-party presidential candidate in the 2016 election.

heat than light. Most tragically, this is true even in the hands of fellow brothers and sisters in Christ.

Smashing the idols of popularity and power

How can Christians best respond to this rancorous climate? Author Tim Keller gives a theological explanation worth our attention: "The increasing political polarization and bitterness we see in U.S. politics today is a sign that we have made political activism into a form of religion."[126] What Keller is talking about is idolatry. According to Rom 1:25, we engage in idolatry any time we worship or serve the creation over the Creator. Anything (or anyone) we give more love, devotion, affection, attention, resources, energy, or concentration to, more so than our creator God, is an idol. When a person hates (or looks condescendingly upon) another person because she is a member of the opposing political party, idol worship is afoot. When a citizen chooses to vote for a candidate solely on the basis of party, so as to achieve victory, and this is more important to the citizen than the politician supporting policies that will bring flourishing to her place, idolatry is likely occurring.

That raises a question: Why is partisan/tribal identity such a potent and persistent idol? Keller poses this analysis:

> The original temptation in the Garden of Eden was to resent the limits God had put on us ("You shall not eat of the tree . . ."; Genesis 2:17) and to seek to be "as God" by taking power over our own destiny. We gave in to this temptation and now it is part of our nature. Rather than accept our finitude and dependence on God, we desperately seek ways to assure ourselves that we still have power over our own lives. But this is an illusion. [Reinhold] Niebuhr believed this cosmic insecurity creates a "will to power" that dominates our social and political relationships.[127]

The shadow side of politics is control: for many people partisanship (consciously or unconsciously) becomes a socially constructed, and tribally enforced power play. And partisanship is fueled by the American ethos of competition: success, achievement—in a word, winning. Regardless of party, everyone likes to win. The renowned pro golfer Walter Hagen famously declared, "No one remembers who came in second."

126. Keller, *Counterfeit Gods*, 100.
127. Keller, *Counterfeit Gods*, 101–2.

When fame and power are pursued through social media posturing and partisan wrangling, the outcome is corrosion and contamination. Both the public square and personal relationships suffer and disintegrate. What can followers of Jesus do to respond constructively?

Of first order: repent. Cast off all pride and humbly beg God to cleanse our craven, insecure, blame-shifting, and self-righteous hearts. Christians don't need popularity or power—in Jesus Christ we are "dearly loved children"[128] who "are more than conquerors."[129] And while the triune God commissions us to earnestly pray for and work for shalom in our world[130] (including for those who may seek to marginalize us), ultimately, our kingdom is not of this world.[131] To live otherwise is to forsake our citizenship and identity in Jesus Christ.

According to Phil 2, the way of life for Christians on earth is one of self-emptying service to the glory of God. Because the Son of God poured himself out for us, we are free to do the same for others. God's redemptive love and inspiring example give Christians the motivation to follow suit.

Our identity in Christ leads to a multitude of rich implications; but most crucially, it means Christians will commit to being the Trinity's peacemakers across this fractured globe. Practically speaking, we will strive to create communities of reconciliation in the places we inhabit. After all, as will be argued in the next chapter, the Church is an icon, or symbol of the Godhead. We represent the loving fellowship of the Trinity to the universe.

Don't be fooled: reconciling has always been a countercultural endeavor. In commenting on 2 Cor 5:18–19, where the Apostle Paul outlines the "ministry" and "message of reconciliation," N. T. Wright asserts,

> Something new *has* happened; something new *must now* happen. The world has never before seen a ministry of reconciliation; it has never before heard a message of reconciliation. No wonder the Corinthians found Paul's work hard to fathom. It didn't fit any preconceived ideas they may have had. He was behaving like someone . . . who lived in a whole new world.[132]

Reconciliation remains a peculiar message and ministry for multiple reasons. As Wright observed, it gestures forward our future in the new heaven

128. 1 John 3:1.

129. Rom 8:37.

130. Jer 29:7.

131. John 18:36; Col 3:1–11; Phil 3:20–21.

132. Wright, *Paul for Everyone: 2 Corinthians*, 65.

and earth. Yet its foundations are eternal: reconciliation is rooted in the nature and character of the Father, Son, and Spirit. As will be seen in the next chapter, the Trinity's inner life and outer mission demonstrate the significance of reconciling in our time.

Questions for Reflection

1. Of the four aspects of place, which one are you most familiar with and why? Which one do you want to investigate further and why?

2. Regarding the Gal 3:28 triad, describe the ways people in your community are divided along the lines of ethnicity, class, and sex. Is one of the three a hot button issue where you live?

3. What role does social media and partisan politics play in your life? How much of your time, talent, and treasure do they occupy? Has either one become an idol?

Practical Next Steps

1. Using the four aspects of place, create a thumbnail sketch of your place or city. Make a list detailing the strengths (Jerusalem) and weaknesses (Babylon).

2. Do a personal examination. If helpful, enlist some safe friends. Is there any ethnocentrism, classism, or sexism in your heart, attitudes, or language? What about a partisan attitude (e.g., reviling the opposite political party/politicians)? Are you spending an excessive amount of time on social media? If so, repent and ask a friend, mentor, or your pastor to hold you accountable, or join a support group.

2 The Foundation: The Relational Nature of the Trinity

UP TO THIS POINT, I've shared my personal quest on the reconciling journey; outlined the four aspects of place, suggested it is wise to interpret place through a tension between sin and grace, discussed the Gal 3:28 triad, and explored the role social media and partisan politics play in exacerbating existing conflicts in our society.

These topics, however, only reveal the zeitgeist of our cultural moment. Jesus beckons his followers to build bridges on a more enduring foundation rather than the shifting tides of broken human societies. Let's return to the analogy of bridge construction.

To construct a bridge

Perhaps the most dominant landmark in Newport is the world-renowned Claiborne Pell (a.k.a. Newport) Bridge. It is a two-mile-long suspension bridge, towering imposingly over Narragansett Bay and the places it links: Newport and Jamestown. On a clear day, any plane can readily see this behemoth from dozens of miles away. It is considered an engineering marvel, requiring 838 steel piles that go 162 feet below the water's surface, rooted into the bottom of the bay.[1] This allowed for the construction of fifty-four piers, created using over ninety thousand cubic yards of concrete, amazingly poured under water.[2] The bridge could not exist without these steel piles and concrete piers. Why?

As mentioned in the opening chapter, most bridges require three interlocking sections: a foundation, a substructure, and a superstructure. Generally speaking, the foundation is composed of anchors (i.e., piles and

1. Muscato, "Newport Bridge."
2. Muscato, "Newport Bridge."

48

piers) that connect the bridge to the underlying ground, whether dry or wet (i.e., seabed). The foundation is the mechanism that stabilizes, and thus makes possible, the entire structure.

Likewise, reconciling requires the most sturdy of foundations. More pointedly, when Christians, a) read the holy Scriptures through a missional narrative, and b) start to explore and comprehend the Trinity's relational being (both God's internal and external nature), they are constructing the best foundation upon which to build bridges of reconciliation in the various hamlets and neighborhoods they inhabit.

Consequently, this chapter takes a sharp turn *away from* place and culture and *toward* the theology of God's being. Admittedly, this could give this section a denser feel than previous ones. I ask for your grace and patience. Here's the crux: if we lack a proper grasp of what underpins reconciling, we will lack the vision and motivation to endure in this calling as reconciling is anchored in the very nature of the Holy Trinity. Finally, this chapter is significant because it lays the groundwork for chapters 3 and 4, which present the substructure and superstructure for those who engage in reconciling.

A specific narrative: the key lens to understanding Scripture

Theologians have established there are numerous ways to interpret the Bible. One is the "Systematic-theological method (STM), which tends to deal with Scripture topically. . . . *The Bible is about God, sin, the Holy Spirit, the church.*"[3] However, I would like to make the case for a narrative reading of the Bible. As a pastor I often hear people describe the Bible "as the story of God" or "the story of Jesus." While correct, many of us would agree they are simplistic. I am proposing you embrace what's called the "missional or missiological" interpretation, defined as "a way of reading the whole of Scripture with mission as its central interest and goal."[4] In this approach, mission is the dominant lens through which the entire Bible is understood. Why? Scholar Martin Kahler argued mission is "the mother of theology," and theology "an accompanying manifestation of the Christian mission."[5] Missiologist Christopher Wright explains:

3. Keller, *Center Church*, 40.

4. Richard Bauckham, quoted in Goheen, *Introducing Christian Mission Today,* 37–38.

5. Kahler, quoted in Bosch, *Transforming Mission,* 16.

A missional hermeneutic of the Bible begins with the Bible's very existence. . . . [T]he whole canon of Scripture is a missional phenomenon in the sense that it witnesses to the self-giving movement of this God toward his creation and us, human beings in God's own image. . . . Furthermore, the processes by which these texts came to be written were often profoundly missional in nature. Many of them emerged out of events or struggles or crises or conflicts in which the people of God engaged with the constantly changing and challenging task of articulating and living out their understanding of God's revelation and redemptive action in the world. . . . The text itself is a product of mission in action.[6]

The reality and development of the Bible validates a missional interpretation.

The missional approach demonstrates some key characteristics. New Testament scholar Richard Bauckham asserts two criteria are essential: 1) "reading the Bible as a whole" and, 2) "one which recognizes how the Bible as a whole tells a story, in some sense a single story."[7] The Bible, from start to finish, forms one cohesive story revealing the mission of the triune God. This concept is termed "a metanarrative": "on this overarching story is based a worldview that, like all worldviews and metanarratives, claims to explain the way things are, how they have come to be so, and what they ultimately will be."[8] In other words, while the Bible is full of stories, each story is a tributary that flows into one, large river.

Before I present my narrative, I want to mention two valid options. The first is "Creation, Fall, Redemption, and Restoration[9]/New Creation."[10] Another example is "a six-act drama: creation, sin, Israel, Christ, church, and new creation."[11] These narratives correctly observe that Scripture begins with creation (Gen 1) and ends with the final creation, the new heaven and earth (Rev 22). They note the effects of sin/the fall on the world. They describe the role of Israel, Jesus Christ, and the Church in God's plan to save the world.

6. Wright, *Mission of God*, 48–49. *Hermeneutics* is a technical word referring to the science of interpreting or understanding texts.

7. Bauckham, *Bible and Mission*, 11–12.

8. Wright, *Mission of God*, 55.

9. Keller, *Center Church*, 43.

10. Tennent, *Invitation to World Missions*, 105.

11. See Bartholomew and Goheen, *Drama of Scripture*. Additionally, a similar model of "Creation, Fall, Israel, Jesus, Church, New Creation" is offered by Woodward and White, *Church as Movement*, 132–35.

However, in this book I am offering a slightly different missional reading. Why? The above narratives reference God as Creator only implicitly. Yet the eternal Creator predates the creation. And so I'm suggesting it is more theologically explicit (and accurate) to start with God's existence. Second, these approaches tend to use language that is more historical (sequential and event based) than relational. In my view, God is fundamentally a relational being: "Scripture and subsequent creeds testify that before the foundation of the world, for all eternity, God has existed in perfect community as Father, Son and Holy Spirit."[12]

Therefore, I am proposing a relational (reconciling) narrative comprising five movements: Creator, first creation, alienation, reconciliation, and final creation. This narrative has multiple strengths. First, it loosely follows a famous text regarding the supremacy of Christ and reconciliation, Col 1:15–23—more on this in chapter 3. Second, it seeks to give reconciliation its proper place as a doctrine that "is central to the Christian faith."[13] And although reconciliation "was never defined by the ecumenical creeds of the Church and remained relatively undeveloped until the Middle Ages," and to the present day there remains no universally accepted definition across all expressions of Christianity, I agree with theologian John W. de Gruchy that it remains a valid narrative, because "all Christian traditions have been shaped by a common foundational narrative of redemption"[14] which is intertwined with reconciliation. One of the main reasons God purchased our freedom was to restore the fractured relationship.

Alright, here we go! The first movement in this reconciling narrative is the Creator: "In the beginning God created . . ."[15] The opening words of Scripture imply a prenarrative, that something—or someone—precedes recorded history. Creation demonstrates the existence and character of the Creator, including "his eternal power and divine nature."[16] Fundamentally, humans would not know God unless God first revealed himself through creation.[17] Because God's first-listed identity is as Creator, consequently,

12. Woodward, *Creating a Missional Culture*, 88.

13. de Gruchy, *Reconciliation*, 47. De Gruchy argues convincingly, "For Paul 'reconciliation' is the controlling metaphor for expressing the gospel" (45) and is "the central theme of Karl Barth's *Church Dogmatics*" (44).

14. de Gruchy, *Reconciliation*, 47–48.

15. Gen 1:1.

16. Rom 1:20.

17. Colin Gunton explains how creation emanates from the Trinity's love and freedom. See Gunton, *Promise of Trinitarian Theology*, 141–45.

"the first word in a mission theology is not 'savior' or 'salvation,' but 'creator' and 'creation.' . . . We often forget that creation is a major theme in salvation."[18] God is eternal, existing outside of time, and holy, transcendent over created matter. The Creator lives independently of the material world yet has revealed his life. How?

That raises a second movement: the first creation. God the Father created everything out of nothing—speaking our world into reality through his son, Jesus Christ, the eternal Word (*logos*)[19] and through the power of the "hovering" Spirit.[20] This world was ordered by natural laws and was "good": lovely and wholesome, bursting with *shalom*—complete delight and flourishing experienced in God's undiluted presence.

Creation points to the all-encompassi8-ng love of the Creator: "The whole message of the Bible is the story of God's love for and relationship with his creation. . . ."[21] God created human beings in his image to exist as social and relational creatures: "We were made for personal and interdependent community with God and his people because we reflect the triune God."[22] Nevertheless, the Trinity's mission is not confined to humankind: God's "ultimate purpose is to draw . . . the entire cosmos into communion with His divine life."[23]

Tragically, communion has been severed. Genesis 3 describes a third movement, an interruption, summarized in Rom 5:12: "sin entered the world through one man, and death through sin." Adam and Eve rebelled against the holy and caring One: "God, by His triune nature, is inherently relational. The fall of man was not merely the entrance of rebellion into the world; it was, at a deeper level, the tragic fracturing of a relationship."[24] More widely, alienation invades the perfection of Eden, and spills over, bringing disharmony, power struggles, violence, decay, pain, suffering, and death into the world. The shared fabric between God, humanity, and earth has been torn and frayed. Conflict and division beset all our relationships:

> The natural human heart wants to be king, and so it is hostile to God's claims of lordship over us. Until we see our instinctive

18. Sunquist, *Understanding Christian Mission*, 184.

19. John 1:1–5.

20. Gen 1:2.

21. Sunquist, *Understanding Christian Mission*, 181.

22. Keller, *Center Church*, 42.

23. Tennent, *Invitation to World Missions*, 177.

24. Tennent, *Invitation to World Missions*, 80.

hostility to God's authority, we can't understand one of the great, deep mainsprings of all human behavior. We are committed to the idea that the only way we will be happy is if we are wholly in charge of our lives. Of course, this self-centered desire to command and control leads to conflict with other human beings. So hostilities with God lead to hostilities with others.[25]

This hostility is as pervasive as a pernicious weed overrunning a garden, or a viral worm infecting the entire network. Put differently, Rwandan pastor Antoine Rutayisire explains there are "four levels of alienation" that simultaneously occur: "man was separated from God, separated from himself (psychological problems), separated from his neighbour (social problems) and separated from nature (ecological problems)."[26] The organism is diseased but not destroyed. God's common grace prevents humans from annihilating everything, and many societies are able to cultivate and maintain a limited measure of order, justice, and growth. Yet the world remains haunted by the distant echoes of Eden, which remind us all is not as it should be.

This leads to the fourth movement: reconciliation. The Godhead initiates a rescue operation where the entire cosmos is to be redeemed and healed. It started when God initiated a covenant with Abraham, who would "bless all peoples on earth"[27] by becoming not only the father of the Jewish nation—who God called to be his "light to the nations"[28]—but also the father of Jesus Christ, the Savior of the world.[29] Jesus came to serve as the "second Adam."[30] Jesus's righteous being, including his words and actions, changes the equation: his conception, birth, sinless life, suffering on the cross, resurrection from the dead, ascension to heaven, outpouring of the promised *paracletos* (Holy Spirit as our advocate and counselor), ongoing ministry of intercession at the right hand of the Father, and future second coming to judge the living and the dead. His reconciling work is multidimensional: his death satisfies the holiness and justice of God, justifies unjust sinners, and conquers the foes of sin, death, and evil.

---

25. Keller, *Hidden Christmas*, 108–9.

26. Rutayisire, "Our Gospel of Reconciliation," in Cameron, *Christ Our Reconciler*, 67.

27. Gen 12:1–3.

28. Isa 49:1–7.

29. Matt 1:1.

30. Rom 5:12–21.

God the Father, Abba, seeks to reunite with and heal the created order, bringing liberation and fullness of life.

The final movement is the new creation, the final "restoration of all things."[31] This total reconciliation is achieved "through" Jesus Christ.[32] At the consummation of the cosmos, there will be complete relational harmony between God, human beings, and creation. Heaven is Eden reconstituted, through a new heaven and earth. It is an environment saturated with love of God, drenched with his glorious presence. The story of ordinary human history concludes with this stirring declaration:

> "Look! God's dwelling place is now among the people, and he will dwell with them. They will be his people, and God himself will be with them and be their God. 'He will wipe every tear from their eyes. There will be no more death' or mourning or crying or pain, for the old order of things has passed away."
>
> He who was seated on the throne said, "I am making everything new!"[33]

In sum, this relational narrative is faithful to the nature of the triune God, the Scriptures, Church tradition, and human experience, and shows how reconciliation occupies the center of the Christian life.

The human role in reconciling

One of the strengths of this relational narrative is that it gives proper emphasis to God's agency—his power, will, and freedom in moving and operating. In mission and reconciling, God is the primary actor. The triune Godhead plans, initiates, and executes God's goal of redeeming and renewing all things. If God does not advance his mission, it will fail.

Yet the relational narrative also makes space for human agency. God, as an act of sheer grace, chooses to invite and empower imperfect human beings[34] to be his co-laborers and ambassadors. So here's the bottom line:

---

31. Acts 3:21.

32. Col 1:20.

33. Rev 21:3–5.

34. First Jews and then Gentiles, the "ingrafted branches." The olive tree comprises both Jews and Gentiles who believe in Jesus Christ. I am not a proponent of replacement theology: that the Church has replaced Israel in God's plan for redemption. See Rom 11:11–32.

the primary agency belongs to God and the secondary agency to humans.[35] While God can reconcile all creation unto the Godhead without human assistance, humans cannot do mission without God's blessing and provision.

Why is this important? First, Christians engage in mission with humility and gratitude. After all, God doesn't actually need us to do what needs to be done. It reminds me of the relationship between my two sons, who are four years apart in age. When Landon invites his younger brother, Kelan, to join an activity with his buddies—whether shooting baskets, riding bikes, or playing video games—Kelan responds with appreciation and enthusiasm. And second, to comprehend God's power and intent in reconciling, we must gain a basic grasp of God's nature—his inner life and outer operations.

The inward Trinity: the source of all is relationship.

The most famous declaration in the Bible is "God is love."[36] But God's loving nature is in danger of being misconstrued by an American culture that tends to sentimentalize love as gushy and saccharine. When we hear the word, we may visualize a heart emoji, or a red velvet box of chocolates, or two people passionately kissing, or a couple holding hands as they stroll down a beach at sunset. But even the purest forms of human love give us just the faintest glimpse of the triune Godhead's relationship. Jesus stated, "Anyone who has seen me has seen the Father. . . . The words I say to you are not just my own. Rather, it is the Father, living in me, who is doing his work. Believe me when I say that I am in the Father and the Father is in me" (John 14:9–11). Jesus continues to use intimate language to describe the relationship between him, the Father, and Holy Spirit from John 14:12 through his high priestly prayer in John 17:26. I encourage you to read it slowly and reflectively as it reveals the profound communal life of the triune God. Tim Keller provides this portrait:

> While there is only one God, within God's being there are three persons—Father, Son and Holy Spirit—who are all equally God and who have loved, adored, served, and enjoyed one another from all eternity. . . . So a triune God created us (John 1:1–4), but he would not have created us to get the joy of mutual love and service, because he already had that. Rather, he created us to share in

---

35. I am purposely omitting the role of angels here.

36. 1 John 4:16.

his love and service. As we know from John 17:20–24, the persons of the Trinity . . . are "other-oriented."[37]

God's relationality is indispensable not only to reconciling, but to theology and mission: "The nature of the Trinity as persons-in-relation is not a subsidiary doctrine or even an attribute of God among others. It is who God is, and it is the very center of Christian theology and therefore of mission."[38]

This calls for us to explore what is sometimes called the "immanent" Trinity: "the Trinity's inner life"[39] or "who God is in his own being."[40] The internal love shared by the Trinity is so complex and profound, theologians developed a technical word for it: *perichoresis*, "the mutually internal abiding and interpenetration of the trinitarian persons."[41]

Pastors J. R. Woodward and Dan White Jr. detail the history and significance of this concept:

> Eastern Orthodox theologians coined the term *perichoresis* in the seventh century to describe the mutual indwelling of Father, Son and Spirit. It's related to our word *choreography*. The dance of God is about the togetherness, the joy, the self-giving, self-surrendering passion and life shared by the Father, Son and Spirit. Jesus described the closeness, saying he is in the Father and the Father is in him (Jn 17:21). God is not a distant, divine, philosophical abstraction but a relational being who invites us into the dance of life—and not just us but the whole creation.[42]

What a breathtaking sight to behold! The Father, Son, and Spirit enjoy a harmonious interdependence. From all eternity, the Trinity has never experienced the frailties and inanities marking all human relations—selfishness, aloofness, misunderstanding, impatience, condescension, etc.

How do we know about God's inner life? Through his "outer" life, known as God's "economy" or the "economic Trinity." Theologian and pastor Ross Hastings describes God's economy as "his actions in creation and redemption. . . . [W]e gain our understanding of the immanent Trinity

---

37. Keller, *Center Church*, 33–34. Colin Gunton agrees: he argues creation emanates from the Trinity's love and freedom. See Gunton, *Promise of Trinitarian Theology*, 141–45.

38. Hastings, *Missional God, Missional Church*, 84.

39. Hastings, *Missional God, Missional Church*, 87.

40. Hastings, *Missional God, Missional Church*, 100.

41. Miroslav Volf, quoted in Hastings, *Missional God, Missional Church*, 274.

42. Woodward and White, *Church as Movement*, 121.

from the revelation of God in Christ by the Spirit."[43] In other words, God's economy is "focused on God's relationship with the world, grounded in the biblical story of creation, redemption, and sanctification."[44] It may be helpful to think of the immanent Trinity as God facing inward, and the economic Trinity as God facing outward.

The inward Trinity and outward Trinity are vital to Christians, congregations, and the wider Church for multiple reasons. First, we join God's inner life through *theosis*, "our union with the triune God in Christ . . . by the Spirit. . . . [W]e are given encouragement to engage in mission as a consequence of who we are in Christ."[45] This means we are defined primarily by an identity granted to us through our union with God. Reconciling then, is rooted in an identity grounded in a relationship, rather than simply an activity we engage in or a "badge" that we wear.

What's more, our identity is not only vertical (our union with God), but it's also horizontal (our union with other Christians) as well. Our lives are undeniably intertwined with the lives of others, that is, our identity as Christians is "a communal or specifically ecclesial reality."[46] Think about it. As God knows, loves, and does mission in community, the Church does the same as it participates in the triune life. The Trinity's inner and outer relations, then, are the center of Christianity. The Church participates in mission and reconciliation inasmuch as it remains relationally connected to the triune God and to one another.

Second, God's nature is a pattern for the Church. Theologians have long indicated that the Church is an icon (image or reflection) of the Trinity.[47] What we observe, through the Scriptures and the eyes of faith, is a dynamic tension between God's internality and externality, his oneness and separateness.[48] God is comprised of three different persons who exist united in one essence as one being. God then, reflects both unity and diversity. And because the Church is united to the Godhead, she too is united and diverse. In its being and identity, the Church is equipped to be an agent

---

43. Hastings, *Missional God, Missional Church*, 100–101.

44. Young, "The Uncontainable God," in Foust et al., *Scandalous Prophet*, 84.

45. Hastings, *Missional God, Missional Church*, 78.

46. Hastings, *Missional God, Missional Church*, 82.

47. I am thinking of Volf, *After Our Likeness*.

48. Hastings uses the words "distinction" and "correspondence." See Hastings, *Missional God, Missional Church*, 101.

of reconciliation because it reflects the life, the character, and both the unity and diversity of the Trinity.

Put in other terms, each local congregation acts as a "hermeneutic of the gospel."[49] That is, Jesus "did not write a book but formed a community."[50] Christianity must not be reduced to an ancient, inscribed religion. Rather, it is a living, dynamic, and diverse witness, a performative sign of God's love. By calling together the disciples, training them, and sending them as apostles, Jesus created the Church, the human community to reveal the divine, triune community to the world. Each local church is to represent the triune God in "its neighborhood[,] . . . the specific place where it lives. . . . [I]t is God's embassy in a specific place."[51]

God's outward-facing roles

In order to for us to grasp our reconciling mission, it is necessary to comprehend the external identities of the Trinity: God the Father is Creator; God the Son is Redeemer; and God the Spirit is the Engine for mission and Reconciler.

God the Creator

In the Scriptures, there are many names and identities for God the Father. For instance, theologians have long argued that the kingdom of God, and thus God's kingship, is the dominant image in the Bible.[52] Here, however, I want to join others[53] in giving more emphasis to God as Creator than King (Sovereign) for several reasons. Fundamentally, humans would not know the

49. Newbigin, *The Gospel in a Pluralist Society*, 222.

50. Newbigin, *The Gospel in a Pluralist Society*, 227. Further, he states that "the center of Jesus's concern was the calling and binding to himself of a living community of men and women who would be the witnesses of what he was and did. The new reality that he introduced into history was to be continued through history in the form of a community, not in the form of a book" (Newbigin, *The Open Secret*, 52).

51. Newbigin, *The Gospel in a Pluralist Society*, 229.

52. Newbigin advanced "the Kingdom of the Father" (Newbigin, *The Open Secret*, 30). Bauckham proposed a "hermeneutic for the kingdom of God" (Bauckham, *Bible and Mission*, 12). Meredith Kline argued that God's roles/identities as Creator and King are tightly interconnected. See Kline, *Kingdom Prologue*.

53. I am aligning myself with the trinitarian missiologies of Scott Sunquist and Timothy Tennent.

trinitarian God unless God had not first revealed his existence through creation. Perhaps this is why the first line of the Apostles' Creed states, "I believe in God, the Father Almighty, creator of heaven and earth."[54]

Second, this emphasis counteracts a prevailing Western dualism between spirit and matter, between saving human souls and caring for the earth, between evangelism and social justice. As Creator, God loves *all* of creation: not just human beings made in his image, but the entirety of the created order. The Trinity's mission is universal: God's "ultimate purpose is to draw . . . the entire cosmos into communion with His divine life."[55]

Third, the Father's role in creation paves the way for a theology of culture, a necessary part of mission. The Creator God invented and, in his sovereignty, oversees culture: "Scripture views God as the author of human culture. God is not a cultural outsider who occasionally intervenes or interrupts the otherwise autonomous process of human history. Rather, Scripture presents God as intimately involved in the world."[56] What is culture? Newbigin described it as "the sum total of ways of living developed by a group of human beings and handed on from generation to generation."[57] He observed culture includes language, art, technology, law, political and social structures, and religion.[58] God formed human beings, who as image bearers create culture together, both intentionally and accidentally. Nations, ethnic groups, and societies are constantly interacting, collaborating, clashing, reacting, and changing. Ultimately, the variety of cultures and subcultures in our world reflects the complexity and diversity of creation, which reflects the will, creativity, and diversity of the Creator.

A personal example may illustrate culture. Each family has a unique subculture: an established set of beliefs, attitudes, habits, etc. I discovered this when my then fiancé and I engaged in premarital counseling months before our wedding. We sought to be proactive in identifying, understanding, and appreciating our differences, especially in regard to family-of-origin issues. (My wife Autumn was a psychology and social work double major. I was a theology major, but almost double majored in philosophy. Can you tell nothing was destined to be decided easily in our family!?)

---

54. Cited in Walt, *Creed*, xviii.

55. Tennent, *Invitation to World Missions*, 177.

56. Tennent, *Invitation to World Missions*, 176.

57. Newbigin, *Foolishness to the Greeks*, 3.

58. Newbigin, *Foolishness to the Greeks*, 3.

Here's some of what we discovered. Although we were born less than two months and forty miles apart, Autumn and I were raised in homes with completely different cultures. Her family consisted of her mother, stepfather, and half-sister. On the other hand, my family was divorced and dispersed—I lived with my mother, step-father, and the younger of my sisters, while my other sister lived two hours away with my father, stepmother, and two half brothers. Autumn's family valued stability and simplicity—they lived in the same house for over thirty years, rarely traveled outside their small county in northwestern Vermont, and remained home during vacations and holidays. In contrast, I lived in seven places between two states (including a tent for the summer due to a mortgage loan snafu) by the time I graduated high school. My family prized constant commotion and adventure: downhill skiing in the winter, visiting family outside Boston during holidays, spending vacations at Williamsburg, Virginia; Disney World, Orlando; or Prince Edward Island, Canada (all driving rather than flying—ugh!). Autumn's family operated according to a routine: dinner every day at 4 PM after school, field hockey or musical rehearsal, homework, TV time, bedtime. My clan's calendar was frenetically packed according to our endless events and activities: Student Council, track and field meets, church youth group activities, lifeguarding shifts at the local pool, my stepfather's computer networking classes, my mom's teaching schedule, etc., etc., etc. Autumn's home was quiet—family members rarely raised their voices. My home was boisterous and demonstrative. When neighbors or friends asked what all the "shouting" was about, we would answer, "We're just having a conversation!"

Thus, during our counseling sessions, we quickly discovered we were bringing two different sets of experiences and expectations (i.e., culture) regarding an "ideal home environment" into our marriage. Autumn was raised in, and therefore craves, a calm, consistent, home-centric atmosphere; alternatively, the Hoffman home exemplified the *Top Gun* flight school: "I . . . have a need . . . a need for speed!" Our upbringings were so dissimilar, to this day, after twenty years of marriage, we still wrestle to integrate our family cultures as we raise our two sons.

And that's the point: cultures need reconciling. While created by humans (with the influence of God), they are mixed entities: they can provide some structure and flourishing, yet remain warped by sin and alienation. Like a car that is not aligned properly, cultures can veer off the road toward the ditch. Only the grace of God, in its various forms, acts as a guardrail that keeps our societies from crashing and exploding. Thankfully, God the Father and Creator conceived and executed a plan to restore the entire cosmos.

Jesus the incarnate Redeemer

That plan is expressed principally through Jesus Christ, the second member of the Holy Trinity and the appointed and anointed Redeemer of all places, peoples, and civilizations. To be clear, the whole Trinity works in concert to renew and liberate culture. I agree with Tim Tennent who maintains the Father is "the source, redeemer, and final goal of culture"; the Son is the "embodiment in human culture"; and the Holy Spirit is "the agent of the new creation."[59] Jesus Christ, however, plays a special role in the Trinity in incarnating (or "enfleshing") God's redemptive strategy. The study of Jesus's identity and role in mission is called "Christology," and may be defined as "reflection on the *person* and *work* of Jesus Christ."[60] As this is an enormous field of study, let's focus on three categories relevant here: the Incarnation, the cross, and the resurrection and ascension.

The Incarnation is God's definitive act of revelation and redemption.[61] Given its complexity, it may be helpful to understand the Incarnation as a cord composed of numerous threads. First, it expresses God's missionary heart: "The incarnation is the character of mission. Everything the church undertakes in the cause of mission must be characterized by a spirit of humility, selflessness, and sacrifice, for these traits characterized Christ's sending."[62] The classic example is Jesus's *kenosis,* his emptying himself of divine glory. Philippians 2:5–8 declares,

> Your attitude should be the same as that of Christ Jesus: Who, be-ing in very nature God, did not consider equality with God some-thing to be to be grasped, but made himself nothing, taking the very nature of a servant, being made in human likeness. And being found in appearance as a man, he humbled himself and became obedient to death—even death on a cross!

59. Tennent, *Invitation to World Missions*, 175–84. In addition, Scott Sunquist states, "The Holy Spirit confronts cultural sin, empowers cultures for change, and draws cultures toward the triune God" (Sunquist, *Understanding Christian Mission*, 252).

60. Bevans and Shroeder, *Constants in Context*, 38, emphasis original.

61. See Heb 1:1–4.

62. Ott and Strauss, *Encountering Theology of Mission*, 105.

Jesus's condescension is stunning: Christ Jesus forfeited equality with God (the splendor and majesty of the divine nature) to become a servant, but not just any servant—a human servant. And this human servant subjected himself to death, but not just any death—the most humiliating and shameful of deaths, death on a cross.

Thus the Incarnation and suffering of Jesus is the example par excellence for all Christians to replicate, and especially those committed to reconciling. The arrival of the suffering servant provides the model and motivation for Christians to build bridges across difference. Jesus willingly left the perfection and ecstasy of the trinitarian fellowship to descend upon this cold, dark, harsh sphere dangling in space. The God who overflows beyond all galaxies—all space, time, and matter—subjected himself to the narrow confines of a womb he created, and patiently endured the tedious process of conception, gestation, labor, and delivery. These facts alone are astonishing. Why?

They demonstrate God's irrepressible love, his unfathomable desire to reunite with his broken and estranged creatures. If God went this far—made this profound a sacrifice to reach out—how can we as Christians excuse doing any less? While we cannot replicate God's selfless act, followers of Jesus can imitate it on a smaller scale in their ordinary lives: by initiating relationships across various barriers, by being fully present, by prayerfully and empathically listening to stories that can be uncomfortable and challenging, by self-examination, by searching for common ground, and by offering generous resources or services if deemed genuinely edifying (not as pity) to the recipient.

A second incarnational thread is Jesus's announcing the arrival of God's reign through his person and presence. At the beginning of his ministry, his first public pronouncement was, "Repent, for the kingdom of heaven is near" (Matt 4:17). Jesus of Nazareth is the corporeal and tangible sign of the triune God's unfolding kingdom. In some magisterial way, the Incarnation is *kairos* (heavenly, eternal time) invading *chronos* (earthly, limited time).[63] God's reign, his new creation is not escapist, not relegated to some distant future, but material and physical in the here and now. It involves God's shalom spreading through the teaching and miracles of Jesus

---

63. Tennent observes, "In the incarnation, Jesus Christ inaugurates the eschaton; the New Creation breaks into the present order" (Tennent, *Invitation to World Missions*, 183).

and his followers. The Incarnation presents a holistic life where proclamation and service, where evangelism and justice are united.[64]

God's embodiment in Christ gestures to a third thread—contextualization: "The Incarnation is the ultimate example of what we call the translatability of the gospel[:] . . . the ability of the gospel to be articulated, received, appropriated, and reproduced into a potentially infinite number of cultural contexts."[65] This shapes cross-cultural mission; because divinity fully inhabited humanity it is possible for the gospel to be communicated and lived out across religious, social, economic, linguistic, political, ethnic, and other barriers. The Incarnation reveals the universal and contextual nature of the gospel.

As the gospel enters each place, however, it acts as a disruptive force, a double-edged sword that affirms and confronts, that soothes and subverts:

> First, the life of Jesus as concretely revealed in real history is God the Father's *validation of the sanctity of human culture*. This should not be viewed as a kind of tangential application of the Incarnation but as central to our understanding . . . of Jesus as fully God and fully man. . . . Second, the life of Jesus as concretely revealed in Jesus of Nazareth provides *the basis for cultural critique*. . . . The Incarnation is the ultimate act of cultural translation. By translating deity into humanity, God enters into our fallen world without compromise.[66]

When God the Son entered fallen creation and implanted himself into a specific setting, he demonstrated its sacredness by inhabiting and enjoying it. Simultaneously, he challenged its corruption by presenting a holy life and dying as a sacrifice for the sins of that locale, and the world.

The final thread is Jesus's perpetual identification with humanity. In a mysterious way, God the Son entered humanity and yoked himself to our experience and nature. Ross Hastings elaborates:

> The Son of God became one with humanity as an ontic entity by his incarnation. He has sisters and brothers because he entered their humanity. The intent of this was that he might be, and vicariously, for humanity. Thus his life was lived vicariously for humanity, his death was the atonement for humanity, his resurrection

---

64. Sunquist states, "Since evangelism is about Jesus, and Jesus was an integrated whole human being, it makes no sense to give a dichotomous reading of Jesus's love for humanity" (Sunquist, *Understanding Christian Mission*, 320).

65. Tennent, *Invitation to World Missions*, 325.

66. Tennent, *Invitation to World Missions*, 179–81.

results in the resurrection of humanity, and his ascension took humanity into the Godhead. He sits at the right hand of the Father as the man for humanity, the one who reigns invisibly over the earth through his church, which is the sign and servant of the kingdom that has already come.[67]

The Incarnation expresses God's love for and personal connection with all humanity, but especially a "solidarity with the poor."[68] It is during the season of Advent that Christians recall Jesus was born into a poor family and worked as a lower-class tradesman and that at his crucifixion, his only possession was a cloak. Upon death, Jesus was buried in a borrowed tomb. Jesus fully identified with the economically deprived class in his society.

A contemporary example of identification comes from John Perkins, the founder of Voice of Calvary Ministries and the Christian Community Development Corporation. As a prominent advocate for social justice, he asserted that reconciliation must be accompanied by two more *r* verbs, *relocation* and *redistribution*: "To minister effectively to the poor I must relocate in the community of need," he writes; and "Christ calls us to share with those in need."[69] Like Christ, the Church disadvantages itself for the sake of the disadvantaged. The desire to do so comes from Christ, who enables the Church's life to interpenetrate the life of the Trinity and so join God's reconciling mission. This union shapes Christians to "become exocentric persons, living our lives to serve the other."[70]

After the Incarnation, the second christological category we are exploring is the cross. The world would never know about the Incarnation except for the cross. Jesus's death and resurrection punctuated the significance of his arrival. The Apostles' Creed states, "I believe in Jesus Christ . . . [who] suffered under Pontius Pilate; was crucified, died and was buried."[71] In 1 Corinthians, the Apostle Paul asserted that theologically speaking, the cross is "of first importance."[72] Indeed the cross inhabited the core of Paul's existence, fueling every fiber of his being: "I want to know Christ—yes, to know the power of his resurrection and participation in his sufferings,

67. Hastings, *Missional God, Missional Church*, 170.

68. Hastings, *Missional God, Missional Church*, 168. The Scriptures indicate God identifies with and defends the poor, i.e., Prov 14:31; 17:5; Ps 140:12.

69. Perkins, *With Justice for All*, 55–56. More on Perkins in chapter 4.

70. Hastings, *Missional God, Missional Church*, 172.

71. Walt, *Creed*, xviii.

72. 1 Cor 15:3.

becoming like him in his death."[73] Authentic Christianity is thoroughly crucicentric: it gives primacy of place to Jesus's sacrifice.

Regarding the cross, I want to accentuate three themes. The first is God's commitment to restoration through sacrifice, or atonement. But as Hastings observes, reconciliation first occurs inwardly:

> While the atonement's substitutionary nature is a reality, the cross event is first and foremost a transaction within the Godhead between the persons of the Godhead. It was devised from the Father (Jn 3:16; 1 Jn 5:8), who sent the Son, who was conceived as to his humanity by the Spirit (Mt 1:20). It was the offering of the Son to the Father by the Spirit.[74]

Many evangelical theologians contend the cross predominantly demonstrates the penal-substitutionary sacrifice of Christ, which means Jesus's death is the sinless sin offering that satisfies God's holy wrath,[75] purchases our freedom from slavery to sin, and brings reconciliation with the triune God.[76] As J. I. Packer noted, there is no separation between the holiness and love of God: "God's love is holy love."[77]

While the meaning of the atonement has been hotly contested in theological circles, owing in large measure to a modern discomfort with the notion of God's wrath, I am raising it here to emphasize the inestimable sacrifice of God. It is impossible for humans to fully grasp the relational, cosmic, spiritual, and physical pain the Son of God willingly endured to reconcile humans to the Godhead. God's love compelled the Father to send his Son in the power of the Spirit, who through the cross and resurrection destroys alienation and thus creates the possibility of divine and human reunion. God values reconciliation *this much*. This reality must not be ignored or caustically dismissed. In fact, if anything, it leads to unabated joy and worship. The prayer "Love Lustres at Calvary" rhapsodizes this response to the atonement: "Help me to adore thee by lips and life. O that my every breath might be ecstatic praise, my every step buoyant with delight, as I see my enemies

---

73. Phil 3:10.

74. Hastings, *Missional God, Missional Church*, 195.

75. The Greek word is *"hilasmos"* or *"hilasterion."* It is sometimes translated "propitiation." See Rom 3:25; Heb 9:5; 1 John 2:2; 4:10.

76. In addition to Hastings, I am thinking of Morris, *Apostolic Preaching of the Cross*, and Stott, *The Cross of Christ*.

77. Packer, *Knowing God*, 122.

crushed, Satan baffled, defeated, destroyed, sin buried in the ocean of reconciling blood, hell's gates closed, heaven's portal open."[78]

That insight leads into the second crucicentric theme: as Christ suffered for reconciliation, so must Christians. "We are not being true to the gospel message if we neglect the place of suffering in mission. The central symbol of Jesus is the cross and the central identity of Jesus in worship is the Lamb and the Eucharist."[79] The passion of Jesus plays a prominent role in all four Gospels.[80] On numerous occasions Jesus indicated his reason for coming to earth was to suffer, die, and rise again, and all disciples are instructed to "deny themselves and take up their cross daily and follow [Jesus]."[81] In response, the early Church adopted the cross as a key identity marker: "from the second century onwards, Christians not only drew, painted and engraved the cross as a pictorial symbol of their faith, but also made the sign of the cross on themselves or others." [82] Christian history bears this out: from the apostles, to the Church fathers, to modern Christian movements, spreading the gospel of the cross has brought suffering, persecution,[83] and even death. It is estimated that currently, tens of millions of Christians across the globe are persecuted for their faith.[84]

Nevertheless, suffering legitimates reconciling faith: "The church is marked by suffering because of our identity with Christ . . . [and] participates in the suffering of Christ in the world."[85] Christ promised his followers would suffer, and the New Testament Epistles confirm that suffering is a sign of God's favor.[86] Unfortunately, for many people in North

78. Bennett, *The Valley of Vision*, 42.

79. Sunquist, *Understanding Christian Mission*, 209.

80. Sunquist asserts the "passion should be understood . . . as the central and defining event of the life of Jesus: a weeklong process of submission to God's will" (Sunquist, *Understanding Christian Mission*, 210).

81. Luke 9:23; see also Mark 8:27–35.

82. Stott, *The Cross of Christ*, 21.

83. Defined here persecution is "various kinds of hostile acts or unjust discriminations by individuals or groups, including both religious and political representatives, which are primarily in response to someone's Christian beliefs or actions" (Tennent, *Invitation to World Missions*, 468).

84. For more info see Open Doors USA, "Christian Persecution."

85. Tennent, *Invitation to World Missions*, 473. Hastings most fully explicates the ideas of theosis and participation. He describes "the knot of Trinity, union and mission" (Hastings, *Missional God, Missional Church*, 248).

86. For example, see 1 Pet 4:13 and Jas 1:1–12.

America and Europe, this is a shocking and countercultural statement. As Tim Keller and others have argued, owing to "moral therapeutic deism" and other forms of late modern and post-Christian spirituality, suffering is considered a curse.[87]

Contrary to these contemporary entrapments, suffering is the smelling salts that awaken Christians to the reality of living "in the constant tension between the 'already' and the 'not yet' of God's rule."[88] In addition to being a sign of the times, suffering also unmasks the existence of evil and demonic forces battling God's kingdom: "suffering vanquishes evil. . . . Blood, as well as the cross, are symbols of the passion and death of Jesus Christ, and here is where the cosmic victory is won. His death is the weapon that defeats all earthly and heavenly powers."[89] Consequently, our trials and travails, illuminate Jesus's passion, resurrection, and victory. As the Church incarnates the hardships of Christ it will experience, in a limited way, his triumph over evil in this age.

A third theme I am highlighting is the prominence of two crucicentric symbols: the Lord's Supper and baptism. These communal ordinances are signifiers that direct the attention of God's people onto the cross and its implications for Christian belief and practice. The Lord's Supper—also known as Holy Communion or the Eucharist, depending on one's theological tradition—clearly and powerfully represents the crucicentric life and unites Christians through remembrance, worship, and participation:

> At the heart of the life of the church is the Eucharistic celebration, in which those who gather around the Lord's table are taken up again and again into his sacrificial action, made partakers of his dying and of his risen life, consecrated afresh to the Father in and through him, and sent out into the world to bear the power of the cross and resurrection through the life of the world. This is how the Eucharist is interpreted in the great consecration prayer (John 17).[90]

Through reenactment, the Eucharist reminds Christians of their union with the triune God through the sacrifice of Jesus Christ. This union leads

87. Keller, *Walking with God through Pain and Suffering*, 57–60.

88. Tennent, *Invitation to World Missions*, 479.

89. Sunquist, *Understanding Christian Mission*, 211–12. Colossians 2:6–15 is the classic text in describing how the cross "disarmed the rulers and authorities."

90. Newbigin, *The Open Secret*, 54. Hastings agrees: "The Eucharist is central and determinative in the gathering" (Hastings, *Missional God, Missional Church*, 211).

to participation in God's mission, which is proclaiming the power of the cross to the world.

Although the meaning of the Lord's Supper varies across Christian traditions[91] and among theologians, for many in Western evangelicalism it carries a more profound meaning than remembrance. Communion includes identity and relationship: "its most essential definition is to do with being, not doing. We take Christ afresh into our being spiritually. In so doing we enter afresh into communion with the triune God: in and through Christ, by the Spirit, to the Father."[92] Furthermore, the eucharistic Supper is a regular communal activity, which can stimulate renewal leading to faithful mission: "as a practice that rehearses the crucial narrative of the Christian faith it forms people who are missional in character and in loving action toward the other. It is missional in that it infuses *hope* within the human participant each time it is taken."[93] Scott Sunquist claims the Eucharist is the glue that binds worship and mission: "If we ignore the importance of this great Eucharistic tradition, we weaken the connection between worship and witness."[94] Significantly, Communion reminds Christians of their identity as a cruciform people: redeemed by God's mission through the cross, they are sent into the world to proclaim and embody its power. Hence, throughout Church history the Lord's Supper has held a prominent role in uniting the Church's inward and outward lives.

Another crucicentric practice is baptism. While I understand and support covenantal views of baptism,[95] I align with Anabaptism in preferring baptism by immersion. In particular, our church reserves this sign for those who have reached the "age of knowledge" (starting at eleven years old), can bear witness to faith in Christ (give a conversion story or testimony), and explain the meaning of baptism. When people ask me to baptize them, I provide this explanation: (1) Jesus did it (Matt 3:13–17), (2) Jesus commanded it (Matt 28:18–20), and (3) it publicly symbolizes our rebirth/salvation (Rom 6:1–4). To be clear: baptism does not save you or guarantee your salvation. Baptism is a symbol. It's meant to publicly show

91. My tradition, Evangelical Friends, hold a symbolic/memorialist view of what we call "communion" (See The Evangelical Friends Church-Eastern Region, *Faith and Practice*, 17).

92. Hastings, *Missional God, Missional Church*, 203.

93. Hastings, *Missional God, Missional Church*, 210, emphasis original.

94. Hastings, *Missional God, Missional Church*.

95. Sometimes called infant baptism, i.e., Presbyterians, Lutherans, Methodists, Nazarenes, etc. Side note: our church practices "child dedication."

the world that you love, trust, and have put your hope in Jesus Christ as Lord and Savior. It also indicates you belong to God's family/body/bride/ the Church. Lastly, it shows you belong to God's new kingdom, which is bringing the new creation. So baptism symbolizes (1) you belong to Christ, (2) you belong to this congregation and the wider (universal) Church, and (3) you belong to God's kingdom and unfolding new creation. Accordingly, baptism points to the relational narrative of Creator, first creation, alienation, reconciliation, and final creation. It is both a solemn and celebratory event that demonstrates one's full commitment to and participation in the life of the triune God and the life of his body—come what may.

Baptism gestures to the third category of Christology: the resurrection and ascension of Jesus Christ. The resurrection of Jesus is well established in Christian tradition. The Apostles' Creed states, "The third day He rose again from the dead."[96] The Apostle Paul argued the resurrection is indispensable to our faith: "If Christ has not been raised, your faith is futile; you are still in your sins. Then those who have fallen asleep in Christ are lost. If only for this life we have hope in Christ, we are to be pitied more than all men."[97]

While the resurrection has been given its due, the doctrine of the ascension has not. David Bryant, the former president of Concerts of Prayer International and chairman of America's National Prayer Committee, contends American evangelicals have neglected the ascension.[98] However, scholar Kevin Giles states that in Lucan (Luke-Acts) theology, the resurrection and ascension act as "two steps" within "one movement."[99] After citing the resurrection, the Apostles' Creed declares, "He ascended into heaven and sits at the right hand of God the Father Almighty. From there, He shall come to judge the living and the dead."[100]

The ascension then, interlinks the Incarnation (first coming) and death of Jesus with his second coming; it connects Immanuel ("God with us"), Savior, and just Judge. How? This event declares Jesus Christ is King of all. Giles comments: "The departure of Jesus into heaven highlights his heavenly reign, completes his earthly ministry and, together with the outpouring of the Holy Spirit, inaugurates 'the last days . . . The ascension is the

---

96. Walt, *Creed*, xviii.

97. 1 Cor 15:17–19.

98. See Bryant, *Christ Is NOW!*, New Providence Publications, or www.ChristNOW. com.

99. Giles, "Ascension," in Green et al., *Dictionary of Jesus and the Gospels*, 48.

100. Walt, *Creed*, xviii.

visible and concrete of expression of Jesus's exalted status."[101] Tim Keller explains: "It is a new enthronement for Jesus, ushering in a new relationship with us and with the whole world."[102] That is to say, Jesus's ascension is akin to the coronation ceremony of a king or queen who climbs the stairs and assumes the throne, a practice found in both ancient and modern monarchies: "The elevation in space symbolized the elevation in authority and relationship. Jesus was tracing out physically what was happening cosmically and spiritually."[103]

The consequences of the ascension are many. First, God the Father demonstrated the supremacy of Christ over all things: "Setting Him at His right hand, the Father ratified, validated, and eternally secured the full redemptive impact of our Lord's incarnation, teachings, healings, sufferings as well as His victories over sin, Satan and death itself."[104] What's more, Christians can have an experiential knowledge of the resurrected Christ because of his ascension: he is "sublimely personal[,] . . . supremely powerful[,] . . . our high priest. . . . He is our intimate, our leader, and our intercessor—on a cosmic scale."[105] For these reasons and numerous others, "The present, ascended status of Jesus is a foundational aspect of the apostolic faith."[106]

Jesus's ascended status as coroneted king has two notable implications: prayer and power. We will discuss the significance and role of prayer in reconciling in chapter 4. For our purposes here, however, I want to highlight Jesus's role as the perfect mediator between God and humanity. Because of the Incarnation, Jesus understands human frailty and failure: "We do not have a high priest who is unable to sympathize with our weaknesses, but we have one who has been tempted in every way, just as we are—yet was without sin."[107] Yet, on the other hand, Jesus overcame sin, evil, and death, and so is uniquely qualified to intercede on our behalf—in fact the only sufficient priest:

> Because Jesus lives forever, he has a permanent priesthood. Therefore he is able to save completely those who come to God through him, because he always lives to intercede for them. Such a high

101. Giles, "Ascension," in Green et al., *Dictionary of Jesus and the Gospels*, 49–50.
102. Keller, *Encounters with Jesus*, 172.
103. Keller, *Encounters with Jesus*, 174.
104. Bryant, "Affirming Christ's Ascension."
105. Keller, *Encounters with Jesus*, 182, 186, 189.
106. Giles, "Ascension," in Green et al., *Dictionary of Jesus and the Gospels*, 46.
107. Heb 4:15.

priest meets our need—one who is holy, blameless, pure, set apart from sinners, exalted above the heavens.[108]

Our high priest was tempted as a human, but never sinned. Now, this person, 100 percent God and 100 percent human, sinless, an all-glorious king, sits at the right hand of Almighty God, hearing our prayers, praises, groaning, and laments, and carrying them to the heart of the Father on our behalf.

Furthermore, our prayers are heard by King Jesus, who is omnipotent: God "exerted [his mighty strength] in Christ when he raised him from the dead and seated him at his right hand in the heavenly realms, far above *all* rule and authority, power and dominion, and *every* title that can be given."[109] Christ has absolute authority over the entire globe: over every political structure, every legal jurisdiction, every financial institution, every mayor, president, and head of state. The power of the ascended and exalted Christ is complete and cosmic!

God's power, when understood and experienced in its richness, offers an unfaltering motivation for those of us who carry a reconciling vision and passion. Christians are able to initiate conversations and friendships with people who are radically different from us because we launch forth from a foundation of Christ's authority. As people redeemed by Jesus Christ, who live in him and whose destinies are "hidden in him,"[110] we remain confident in God's ability to execute his perfect plan for our lives, including the intricate web of relationships we're attached to. Of course, our attitude is always tempered by human frailty. Strength and weakness exist in paradox. Christians comprehend that although "outwardly we are wasting away, inwardly, we are being renewed day by day,"[111] and "when I am weak, then I am strong."[112] Struggle, and even seeming decline bring sharper relief and vividness to God's excellencies, which glow through the fractures in these "cracked pots," aka, our human bodies.[113]

How does the reconciling Savior shine through us? The ascended one sent the "Spirit of Jesus,"[114] the Holy Spirit, to inhabit God's royal children, his princes and princesses. The Spirit speaks, convicts, empowers, and

108. Heb 7:24–26.

109. Eph 1:20–21, emphasis mine.

110. Col 3:3.

111. 2 Cor 4:16.

112. 2 Cor 12:10.

113. 2 Cor 4:7.

114. Acts 16:7.

teaches Christians of the authority vested in them to serve as peacemakers in all places they reside, influence, or visit. The Spirit helps Christians realize they represent the King's reign and reconciling will.

The Spirit is Mission Leader and Reconciler

In much of Western Christianity, the third member of the Holy Trinity has often been ignored or overhyped. After devoting two lines to God the Father, and nine lines to Jesus Christ, the Apostles' Creed spares six words for the Spirit: "I believe in the Holy Spirit."[115] Although interest in the Holy Spirit reemerged with the explosive rise of Pentecostalism during the twentieth century, in my experience, evangelicals tend to neglect the role of the Holy Spirit in the reconciling mission of the Church.[116] Thus the following section seeks to present a minor corrective to this trend.

Starting in Acts 2, at Pentecost, the Holy Spirit moves to the forefront of Christian mission. Allow me to sketch out the first half of Acts: the Spirit empowers bold witness,[117] "strengthened, encouraged, and grew" the Church throughout Judea, Galilee, and Samaria (Acts 9:31), and revealed to the Apostle Peter that the Gentiles have received him and thus are to be included in the Church (Acts 10–11). The Spirit set apart and sent out Saul and Barnabas to preach the gospel in Cyprus and beyond (Acts 13), and guided the apostles and elders in making a determination at the Jerusalem Council regarding the four "requirements" under which the Gentiles could join the Church and have fellowship with Jewish Christians (Acts 15:22–29). The "Spirit of Jesus" directed Paul's steps, blocking him from Bithynia and redirecting him toward Macedonia (Acts 16:6–10).

This is the reason why Lesslie Newbigin claims, "It is the Spirit who is the witness. . . . It is he who is, properly speaking, the missionary."[118] Consequently, he labels the third member of the Trinity as "the Sovereign Spirit,"[119] and refers to "the sovereign activity" and "sovereign government"[120] of the

---

115. Walt, *Creed*, xviii. Thankfully, the final section of the Nicene Creed devotes around thirty-two words (in English) to the person of the Holy Spirit.

116. A portion of my PhD thesis was devoted to addressing Tim Keller's underdeveloped theology of the Spirit in mission. See Hoffman, "A Critical Assessment."

117. See Acts 2:4; 4:31; 6:5–10; etc.

118. Newbigin, *Trinitarian Doctrine for Today's Mission*, 40.

119. Newbigin, *The Open Secret*, 20, 56, 58.

120. Newbigin, *Trinitarian Doctrine for Today's Mission*, 50.

Spirit, along with "the rule of the Spirit" and "the regime of the Spirit."[121] In his view the Church

> is not in control of the mission. Another is in control, and his fresh works will repeatedly surprise the church, compelling it to stop talking and to listen. Because the Spirit himself is sovereign over the mission, the church can only be the attentive servant. In sober truth the Spirit is himself the witness who goes before the church in its missionary journey. The church's witness is secondary and derivative. The church is witness insofar as it follows obediently where the Spirit leads.[122]

Is Newbigin exaggerating? The answer is not in the least, if we consider the role of the Spirit in Jesus's ministry and subsequent mission of the Church. The Spirit sent Jesus on mission by initiating his conception, anointing him at his baptism, bringing him to his temptation in the desert, and launching his ministry afterward.[123] Even Jesus's first sermon indicated the Spirit set him apart for this work.[124]

What was true of Jesus is true of his Church. God's people, scattered as individuals and gathered as congregations, are a Spirit-birthed, Spirit-infused, and Spirit-led community. Through the constant indwelling presence of the Spirit, the Church points to God's kingdom "as cash in advance[,] . . . a foretaste of the messianic feast[,] . . . a real presence of the love, joy and peace that belong to God's perfect reign."[125] God's people don't simply do missions or evangelism; our very being and identity is rooted in the Spirit.

The Spirit operates inside and outside the Church in multifaceted ways. Scripture indicates the Spirit (1) purifies, (2) unifies, (3) empowers, and (4) prepares the way for the Church. First, the Holy Spirit works inside the Church to bring holiness, which is a dynamic process: it is both individual and communal, both negative (the mortification of sin) and positive (growing in Christlikeness). It involves an inner transformation of heart, mind, and being that is expressed outwardly through ethical living.[126] Fundamentally holiness is "about love in all its fullness."[127] This means the Spirit

---

121. Newbigin, *The Open Secret*, 63.

122. Newbigin, *The Open Secret*, 61.

123. Luke 1:35; 3:22; 4:1; and 4:14, respectively.

124. Luke 4:18.

125. Newbigin, *The Open Secret*, 62.

126. See the fruit of the Spirit in Gal 5:22–23.

127. Brower Latz, "The Dynamic of Holiness," in Davenport, *Conversations on*

washes the motives and attitudes of reconcilers, removing the barriers of arrogance, prejudice, defensiveness, suspicion, and division.

This same Spirit unifies the body of Christ. The Church, comprising God's redeemed sinners, is bound together through its union to the Father through Christ in the Spirit. Theologian Keith Warrington points to the nine "ones" of Eph 4, which indicate Christians possess "a unity that has already been initiated (4:3) and is characterized by the Spirit (4:4). They are to maintain and guard that unity consistently and continuously in their relationships with one another because of, and with the help of, the Spirit."[128]

While our unity in the Spirit is real, Christians must still rely on the Spirit to perpetuate this union visibly to the world. This is why our church, EFC Newport, is intentional in catalyzing various activities that foster unity in the body of Christ, including monthly prayer meetings with other churches, hosting conferences and trainings, and initiating collaborative outreach events. For instance, over three years,[129] EFC Newport served as the primary catalyst behind the New England Festival of Hope. The purpose of this festival was to (a) share the gospel with those who do not identify as Christians or are dechurched (attend church twice a year or less) and (b) demonstrate the unity and diversity of the church in New England. The festival brought churches of diverse denominational, ethnic, class, and theological backgrounds together, showing our diversity and unity in Christ. The Church in our region is a lovely mosaic!

In the first year, five congregations participated, but by our third year, fourteen congregations from three states were involved. Churches could become a "partner" church by committing to at least two out of three activities: (1) praying for the festival, (2) promoting the festival, and (3) financially supporting the festival. It was held at Easton's Beach, one of Newport's most famous beaches. There was live music, cotton candy, activities for the children (e.g., face painting or making crafts), a Christian testimony given by Red Sox baseball greats (Bill Buckner, Trot Nixon, and Dwight Evans, respectively), and a BMX, dirt-bike demonstration by X Games legend Kevin Robinson, who holds several bike-jumping records (gravity-defying and heart-stopping stuff!). After each event, a multi-church prayer team was trained to minister to people and then follow up with them. And the promotional materials gave equal credit to each

---

Holiness, 18.

128. Warrington, *The Message of the Holy Spirit*, 224.

129. From 2014 to 2016.

participating church, whatever their role.[130] It was breathtaking and exhilarating to have dozens of Christians from numerous churches praying, planning, serving and worshipping together in a public space.[131]

Third, the Spirit empowers the Church: "The Holy Spirit inspires bold proclamation (Acts 4:8–31) and clear teaching about Jesus Christ . . . the Holy Spirit *brings power*: power for transformation, for working miracles and healing, for clear and strong preaching, and for obedience to the law."[132] Another example is spiritual gifts, as described in 1 Cor 12, Rom 12, and Eph 4. Spirit-led communities will make an effort to cultivate these gifts. In doing so, because these *charismata* (free gifts) are for everyone, and not given based on ethnicity, education, class, or sex, the Church will stand out as a subversive force in a hierarchical world. Indeed, spiritual gifts are another way the body of Christ reflects the unity and diversity of the Trinity, because, like God, although we "form one body," there are "many parts."[133] EFC Newport regularly teaches on spiritual gifts, encourages congregants to take online tests for those unsure of their gifts, and we offer people the freedom to explore serving in different ministries through trial-and-error, and if an activity (say teaching in our children's ministry) is not a good fit, he/she can try something different.

Finally, the Spirit works preveniently: he "always goes before the church in its missionary journey."[134] In particular, the Spirit is working in people who may appear to have no faith or those with other religious commitments, including Muslims, Hindus, and Buddhists who "had some definite experience of the Holy Spirit *before* they were Christian. Some had reoccurring dreams call them to Jesus, some had a demon cast out, and one had a vision of heaven."[135]

130. For more info on the New England Festival of Hope check out these articles: Flynn, "Hundreds gather at Festival of Hope," and Elsworth, "Newport's Festival of Hope."

131. Unfortunately, after 2016 we discontinued the annual event as everyone needed a break and some key volunteers moved away. You can obtain info on the public Facebook page: https://www.facebook.com/nefestivalofhope/?eid=ARC8ZLpIUhxKv03zYyl mgDm6cmo6v4PsgDXJ_E_gQsnvVghXmmw0FiNEJIN-iSdKgQnM41jipRxBrTPf.

132. Sunquist, *Understanding Christian Mission*, 235–37.

133. 1 Cor 12:12.

134. Newbigin, *The Open Secret*, 56. He states, "The true evangelist knows that the faith of these new Christians is not the effect of which his words were the cause; he knows that his words were but instruments of the work of the Spirit, a work which began before he arrived and continues after he left, of which their faith is the fruit" (Newbigin, *Trinitarian Doctrine for Today's Mission*, 36).

135. Sunquist, *Understanding Christian Mission*, 260, emphasis original.

What do these activities of the Spirit mean for reconcilers? To learn to depend on the Holy Spirit more. In practical terms this may lead to less strategizing and more seeking: "Empowerment for mission is more about prayer, devotion, and silence than about fundraising and seminars. . . . Our doctrine of the Holy Spirit requires that we wait, listen, and respond to the Spirit's prompting."[136] Although this is challenging (especially for me, an Enneagram 3 achiever and doer!), we do so in obedience to Jesus: "Jesus's first command in mission is not to go, but to wait (Acts 1:4). . . . The secret to the spiritual life, and therefore to the missional existence, is to wait for the Holy Spirit . . . [to be] watchful and alert towards others and toward God's Spirit.[137]

Prayer, however, does not preclude study. Reconcilers will carefully research their place and the people inhabiting it, so as to contextualize the gospel. Yet we must be cautious: we live in a culture that is obsessed with analytics, market testing, and the metrics of success—numerical growth. Nevertheless, the sovereign Spirit remains the primary missionary. And because reconciling originates in the heart of God, and the Trinity is on mission, the Church will be wise to slow its pace in order to be attentive to the Holy Spirit.

The reconciling Spirit

God the Father sent God the Son to initiate reunion with creation; then Jesus sent the Spirit to implement Christ's reconciling work. Thus the Holy Spirit is nothing less than "the Spirit of reconciliation"[138]: "God in Jesus Christ *through* the Holy Spirit is reconciling the world to himself, restoring 'all things.'"[139] Amos Yong contends, "the goal of Christian mission is the reconciliation of the world in all of its complexity to God through Jesus

---

136. Sunquist, *Understanding Christian Mission*, 239.

137. Sunquist, *Understanding Christian Mission*, 400, 405.

138. Kim, *Holy Spirit in the World*, 170–81. She draws this conception predominantly from the Apostle Paul's theology and the World Council of Churches conferences in Canberra (1991) and Athens (2005). Kim states, "Canberra connected the reconciling ministry of Jesus Christ and the ministry of the church within the ministry of the Spirit, which is reconciliation. . . . In focusing attention on the Spirit's role as healer and reconciler, the Athens conference . . . encouraged a comprehensive understanding of the Holy Spirit's work" (*Holy Spirit in the World*, 179).

139. Snyder, *Yes in Christ*, 19, emphasis mine.

Christ *by the power* of the Holy Spirit."[140] Christians and congregations, then, will be intentional in joining the Spirit in restoring and renewing the fractured relations between the Creator and creation.

To further underscore this point, I want to present three characteristics of the reconciling Spirit, which will help reconcilers identify and rally around the work of the Spirit.

First, the Spirit is *dynamic*. The Scriptures describe the Spirit by using "the Hebrew word *ruach* and the Greek word *pneuma* . . . they can be translated as 'wind,' 'storm,' 'breeze,' etc. . . . or 'breath.'"[141] These images convey the vibrancy of the Holy Spirit, that is, God "is a breathing, living, acting God."[142] Jonathan Edwards noted, "The Spirit is the river of the water of life, which in heaven proceeds from the throne of God and of the Lamb (Rev. 22:1)."[143] More expressively, Michael Goheen asserts, "The Spirit is like a powerful river of kingdom salvation that flows from the work of Jesus as the source to the ends of the earth, carrying the church along in its eschatological current."[144] "River" and "current" are explicitly biblical and ecological, pointing to God as Creator, both of the first and final creations.

Because this river flows everywhere over the earth the dynamic Spirit is omnipresent. Irenaeus observed the Spirit "was sent *in omnem terram*—'into the whole of the earth.'"[145] Consequently, the Spirit moves equally inside and outside the Church, in the so-called "sacred" and the "secular." Orthodox theologian Georges Fedotov suggests the Spirit "is active in the dynamism of the cosmos and in the inspiration of everyone who creates beauty."[146]

What does that look like? The Spirit is simultaneously universal and particular. He carries the reconciling message of the cross to specific people in particular places all over the world, whether to agnostics in Copenhagen, Denmark, to Hindus in Kolkata, India, or to Buddhists in Kathmandu, Nepal. The Spirit's reconciling ministry addresses the whole person in his or her environment: it "emphasizes the affective, imaginative, and narrative aspects of human rationality . . . [it is] relational,

---

140. Yong, *The Missiological Spirit*, 14, emphasis mine.

141. Berkhof, *Doctrine of the Holy Spirit*, 13.

142. Berkhof, *Doctrine of the Holy Spirit*.

143. Jonathan Edwards cited in Thiselton, *The Holy Spirit*, 288.

144. Goheen, *Introducing Christian Mission Today*, 101.

145. Congar, *I Believe in the Holy Spirit*, 219, emphasis original.

146. Congar, *I Believe in the Holy Spirit*, 219.

interpersonal, and even intersubjective, enabling people to touch each other in the core of their beings."[147] The Spirit touches the deepest parts of humans and allows them to connect meaningfully.

The dynamic Spirit is not only omnipresent but also the eternal one who *bridges* time and eternity. The Holy Spirit bookends the Protestant canon. In Gen 1, at the beginning of the first creation, "the Spirit of God was hovering over the waters."[148] Fast forward to the unveiling of the final creation in Rev 22: "The Spirit and the bride say, 'Come!' . . . Let the one who is thirsty come; and the let the one who wishes take the free gift of the water of life."[149] Because the eternal Spirit spans the first and final creation, "Through the Spirit of Christ [Christians] . . . become participators in the eschatological history of the new creation."[150] Said differently, the Spirit is "the anticipation of the end in the present."[151] The Spirit indwells Christians, both individually and corporately (through local congregations) and serves as a deposit, foretaste, and sign of our eternal and materially perfect future. We can reconcile with courage, peace, and joy, because we experience now what the end of time is like. The Spirit strengthens us by reminding us the victory is won and our glorious future in heaven has been secured in Christ and so we can serve others with unhindered freedom and love.

A second characteristic of the Spirit is *boundary-breaker*.[152] The Spirit brings revolution by disrupting traditional and exclusionary boundaries. Two stories from the book of Acts provide us with ample evidence. The first is Acts 2, at Pentecost, where the Spirit is poured out on the 120 in Jerusalem. This is a watershed event whereby a new, Spirit-led age manifests, one that disrupts and overturns systems of injustice.[153] In explaining this supernatural and confusing occurrence, the Apostle Peter quotes Joel 2:28–32, which is "an explicit reference to the democratization of the Spirit in the last days. It is no longer a small chosen group of people to experience the Spirit, but 'sons' and 'daughters,' old men and young men,

---

147. Yong, *The Missiological Spirit*, 229.

148. Gen 1:2.

149. Rev 22:17.

150. Moltmann, *Trinity and the Kingdom*, 90.

151. Oscar Cullmann quoted in Thiselton, *The Holy Spirit*, 344.

152. Theologians sometimes use the term *iconoclastic*. See Hoffman, "The Missiological Debate Over Acts 2:14–21."

153. Willie James Jennings states, "The Holy Spirit presents a profoundly counterhegemonic reality" (Jennings, *The Christian Imagination*, 266).

and male and female slaves. . . . It implies God's calling upon them for service."[154] Amos Yong elaborates:

> The Spirit actually overturned the status quo . . . those at the bottom of the social ladder—women, youth, and slaves—would be recipients of the Spirit and vehicles of the Spirit's empowerment. People previously divided by language, ethnicity, culture, nationality, gender, and class would be reconciled in this new version of the kingdom.[155]

At Pentecost, the Holy Spirit (spiritually) crashed the hierarchical system in Roman-controlled first-century Israel. God's kingdom breaks into history and shines as an alternate society, whereby those marginalized by dominant elites are now equally gifted and empowered to proclaim and embody the gospel. This occurs through the reconciling work of the Holy Spirit, who in this new age, breaks down entrenched norms and rules to create a new community, one that is diverse, yet united through the crucifixion and resurrection of Jesus Christ (Acts 2:29–36).

Pentecostal theologian Keith Warrington presents a similar idea but uses different language. In his view, the Spirit creates radical inclusion, which honors difference while simultaneously fostering unity:

> The Spirit is interested in inclusion, providing an opportunity for unique cooperation and harmony. Thus, he initiates a community that includes women, men and children, young and old, multiracial, culturally varied and nationally diverse. The church, as initiated by the Spirit, is a medley of people who are privileged to stand with each other, to relate to each other, to minister together on behalf of the Spirit and thus to reflect God and his purposes.[156]

Additionally, Warrington contends the "phenomenon of tongues . . . may be viewed as a reversal of Babel. There, language became the reason for the disintegration of the society, whereas now, in the initiation of the church, a reconstitution of history by the Spirit has occurred."[157] At Pentecost, the Spirit overturns the linguistic and ethnic divisions established at the tower of Babel (Gen 11:1–9) through the formation of the Church, a diverse, yet inclusive community in which people share in fellowship, mission to the nations, and

---

154. Ma and Ma, *Mission in the Spirit*, 50.

155. Yong, *Who Is the Holy Spirit?*, 14–15.

156. Warrington, *The Message of the Holy Spirit*, 141.

157. Warrington, *The Message of the Holy Spirit*, 140–41.

the ultimate goal of glorifying God. The Spirit has replaced the old order with a new one that reflects the values of the kingdom of God.

The arrival of this new order is confirmed by a profound and personal story, depicted in Acts 10–11.[158] It starts when the Spirit arranges a meeting between two radically opposite people: Cornelius and Peter. At this seminal event, the reconciling Spirit appears (through an angel) to Cornelius (a God-fearing, Gentile military officer) and simultaneously, to Peter (the Jewish leader of the outcast church in Jerusalem) in a vision revealing God's love for the Gentiles.[159] Cornelius sends three trusted confidants to Peter's house in Jerusalem. The following day, the four men travel to Cornelius's house in Caesarea. Upon their arrival, a consequential dialogue ensues. Then the Holy Spirit comes in power and all present commit to faith in Jesus Christ and are baptized. This incident breaks barriers on multiple levels: "this is the story not only of the conversion of Cornelius but also of the conversion of Peter and of the church . . . mission changes not only the world but also the church."[160]

From here on, mission expands rapidly to the responsive Gentiles. Importantly, in Acts 15, the apostles gather for the Jerusalem Council where the Gentiles' requirements for entry and fellowship into the Church are set.[161] The disruptive effects of Spirit on the world and the Church cannot be overstated. Exclusive walls are wrecked by the inclusion the Spirit ushers in.

To recap, the sovereign, reconciling Spirit directs mission. He is the fuel, engine, and navigator of mission. He prepared and launched Jesus into ministry. He purifies, unifies, empowers, and paves the way for the Church. The reconciling Spirit renews the fractured created order, reuniting it with God through a ministry that is dynamic and boundary breaking. The Spirit flows as a mighty river that confronts the unjust people and systems of our dark age. The Spirit also streams into the Church and world, washing it with God's healing shalom, carried from the reservoir of heaven, until the consummation of all things.

---

158. Christopher Wright observes, "The mere fact that Luke devotes two chapters to tell the story and then to repeat it indicates how pivotal it was in his narrative" (Wright, *The Mission of God*, 515).

159. "I now realize how true it is that God does not show favoritism but accepts from every nation the one who fears him and does what is right" (Acts 10:34–35).

160. Newbigin, *The Open Secret*, 59.

161. Acts 15:1–35.

Conclusion

Reconciling is animated by a relational reading of Scripture, one that expresses a five-part plotline: Creator, first creation, alienation, reconciliation, and final creation. This means relationality is a significant theme in the Scriptures. The triune Godhead, a being in communion, crafted the cosmos out of the overflow of his love and communion. For reasons known only to him, God chose to create more beings for him to love, and to reciprocate that love in return. This narrative includes the inward-facing Trinity: the perfect harmony and mutual service shared among the three members of the Godhead. Hence the triune God is the model, source, and motivation for reconciling.

Yet God is also outward facing: at the appointed time, the Trinity sprung into action, and implemented God's eternal plan to reverse the effects of sin and alienation. This means God the Father is Creator, Jesus is the incarnate Redeemer, and the Holy Spirit is Mission Leader and Reconciler. The Father sent the Son to the cross in order to liberate the world from its bondage to death, sin, decay, evil, and alienation. Then, the resurrected, ascended, and enthroned King sent the Holy Spirit to implement and fulfill this mission, culminating in a new heaven and earth—all is restored and reunited with God. Thankfully, the Spirit advances this mission through Christians and congregations who answer the call by embracing the message, ministry, and identity of reconciliation as part of the new creation in Christ. To that topic we now turn our attention.

Questions for Reflection

1. What are your thoughts concerning the relational narrative of Creator, first creation, alienation, reconciliation, and final creation? Do you agree with it and find it helpful? If not, how would you modify it?

2. Regarding the inward-facing nature of the Trinity and the outward-facing nature of the Trinity, which are you more comfortable with and why?

3. Prior to reading this chapter, what did you know about the Holy Spirit? How has this section given you new information or challenged your thinking?

Practical Next Steps

1. Spend at least one week reading John 14–17 carefully. Jot down your observations in a journal. How do the Father, Son, and Holy Spirit relate to one another? How do they work together for mission?

2. Interview your pastor regarding his/her views of Communion and baptism. Ask how these practices reveal the Trinity's reconciling mission.

3. Take some time to further investigate the sovereign and reconciling Holy Spirit. Identify a few areas in your life or witness where you need more of his empowerment for reconciling. Every day ask the Spirit to lead you to the people and situations where he would have you be a bridge-builder across difference.

3 The Substructure: Reconciling Theology

THE SECOND ESSENTIAL SECTION of a bridge is the substructure. It is perhaps the least noticeable part of the bridge, when compared to the piers/ legs below, and the towers and cables above. Yet the substructure remains indispensible for two reasons. First, it acts as the glue or connective tissue that binds the foundation and superstructure together. Second, it acts as a buffer that disperses the weight (and the pressure it creates) between the superstructure on top, and the foundation below.[1]

So let's review by returning to our crowning analogy: reconciling is like building bridges across difference. Reconcilers must start with a strong foundation, one that is grounded in the relational nature of the Trinity. That brings us to a theology of reconciliation, which acts as the substructure in this paradigm. Having explored God's nature, it is vital to examine human nature. In particular, we turn our attention to how the reconciling God views humans. That is, reconcilers are called to adopt God's lens or perspective, which I am calling "the four great equalizers." These concepts call reconcilers to adopt four postures toward all people.

Please believe me when I say these equalizers and postures matter— they have real-life, practical implications. In fact, I wish I had a better grasp of them back in 2013, when I was party to a painful and serious church conflict that could have destroyed my calling and career. By the way, does that admission capture your interest? I hope so, because I will circle back to this incident at the end of this chapter. Let's press forward to explore what information could have proved helpful.

---

1. See History of Bridges, "Structure, Components and Parts of Bridge."

The imago Dei

The first great equalizer is the doctrine of the *imago Dei*, or "image of God," which indicates all humans are made in the likeness of God.[2] God creates all humans to be in relationship with his triune being—there are no favorites. Each human is a representation of God in miniature and of identical worth. From our Creator's perspective, there is no superior or inferior sex, ethnicity, class, etc. In fact, God forbids murder and violence due to the value conferred on humans because of the *imago Dei*: "Whoever sheds the blood of man, by man shall his blood be shed; for in the image of God has God made man" (Gen 9:6). Thus every human being, even if considered atypical by normal standards (e.g., Down Syndrome, dwarfism, or autism spectrum disorders), is equal in importance and dignity. Think about that. Every human is carefully designed and crafted by God, to reflect his beauty, and has the potential to have an intimate relationship with him. C. S. Lewis, when referring to each human's "potential glory hereafter," famously penned, "There are no *ordinary* people. You have never talked to a mere mortal. Nations, cultures, arts, civilization—these are mortal. . . . But it is immortals whom we joke with, work with, marry, snub, and exploit—immortal horrors or everlasting splendors."[3]

The tragedy is that humans do not share God's heart and vision. Instead, we demean and exclude each other by creating walls: castes, classes, social pecking orders, and hierarchies. We assign some higher or lower worth based on characteristics such as skin pigmentation, location, ancestry, and economic output. Why?

Universal human sinfulness and the brokenness of creation

The answer is found in the second great equalizer, human sinfulness. Every person is afflicted by sin; each is born with a fallen nature. The Apostle Paul pounds this drum repeatedly in Rom 1–3, culminating in these stark declarations: "Jews and Gentiles alike are all under sin. As it is written: 'There is no one righteous, not even one.' . . . There is no difference, for all have sinned and fall short of the glory of God."[4] Sin is not to be trifled with, laughed at, or waved off. It is pervasive and destructive. We know this

2. Gen 1:26–27.

3. Lewis, *The Weight of Glory*, 45–46, emphasis original.

4. Rom 3:9–10, 23.

because the Old Testament offers three predominant word images for sin. They give us insight into how sin infects and infiltrates our lives and world. Psalm 32:1–2 contains all three: "How blessed is he whose *transgression* is forgiven, Whose *sin* is covered! How blessed is the man to whom the LORD does not impute *iniquity*."[5]

Let's start with sin ("Whose sin is covered"), which conveys "the idea of *missing the mark*."[6] This image connotes being "lost" or "going astray."[7] Because sin cracks and distorts our spiritual compass, humans are unable to locate and faithfully follow the right coordinates. Instead we are disoriented, and cannot find our way home—the presence of the living God.

Another significant picture is "'transgression', or a stepping over a boundary."[8] When humans sin they violate God's holy character as outlined in his law. In other words, sin is crossing God's boundaries as established in the Scriptures. Christian psychologists Drs. Henry Cloud and John Townsend helpfully explain that boundaries are rooted in "the very nature of God. God defines himself as a distinct, separate being, and he is responsible for himself. He defines and takes responsibility for his personality by telling us what he thinks, feels, plans, allows, will not allow, likes, and dislikes."[9]

For example, the Ten Commandments tell us it is morally wrong to murder, commit adultery, steal, lie, and covet.[10] Sin is deeply social. It not only offends the relational God, but also harms persons made in his image and with whom we are instructed to share a common life, space, and resources. This is precisely why Jesus, when asked which of the commandments was "most important," intertwined our love of God with love of neighbor.[11]

This understanding of sin often challenges Western cultural notions of personal autonomy and individual rights. We live in an age characterized by radical individualism and post-institutionalism.[12] That means many of us prioritize self-expression/actualization and individual choice before communal or familial commitments. Resultantly, many people try to detach from social or societal commitments that would benefit them

---

5. Ps 32:1–2 NASB, emphasis mine.

6. Kevan, *What the Scriptures Teach*, 14, emphasis original.

7. Ps 119:176; Isa 53:6.

8. Kevan, *What the Scriptures Teach*, 14.

9. Cloud and Townsend, *Boundaries*, 32.

10. Exod 20:13–17.

11. Mark 12:28–34.

12. For more on this see Putnam, *Bowling Alone*.

and others. An illustration of this phenomenon is "the nones," those adults who do not affiliate with any religious group. As of 2019 they are the largest religious group in the US at 23.1 percent, slightly larger than Catholics (23 percent) and evangelicals (22.5 percent). [13] In increasing measure, Americans are resisting identifying with or committing to a specific religious organization or institution.

A third image for sin is "*iniquity . . .* [which] means crookedness, perversion, or distortion. It is the opposite of being straight or upright, and it indicates that what was originally erect has become bent or twisted."[14] Perhaps this is the easiest image of sin for modern people to grasp. Many of us have had the experience of playing tennis or racquet ball with a warped (but usable) racket, or driving a car with a bent tire rim, or crooked alignment. In both cases, the natural trajectory of the ball or car is off, and we sense the instability and inconsistency.

The bottom line: all humans are equal in the sight of God because they're universally afflicted by sin. According to Rom 3, each and every person is in bondage to sin, is unable to please God, is legally guilty, and thus stands condemned before the only just Judge. It's no surprise then, that they are relationally alienated from their Maker. It's a grim condition indeed.

Having said that now is an appropriate moment to hit the "pause" button and offer a caveat regarding "total depravity." For many Christians, this doctrine has been presented in a way that is clumsy, heavy-handed, or exaggerated almost to the point of being grotesque. All is not lost. Our sin is not greater than God's righteousness poured out through Jesus Christ.[15] Humans still contain a vestige of the *imago Dei*. God's common grace keeps most societies from devolving into total barbarism, anarchy, and violence. The world is not as degenerate as it fully could be. R. C. Sproul states, "Total depravity is not utter depravity. We are not as wicked as we possibly could be."[16] I want to qualify our discussion of sin by quoting theologian Donald Bloesch, who argues total depravity has "four meanings":

13. Jenkins, "'Nones.'"

14. Kevan, *What the Scriptures Teach*, 16, emphasis original.

15. See Rom 5:15–17.

16. Sproul, *Essentials Truths*, 149. For this reason, Sproul states, "Perhaps *radical corruption* is a better term to describe our fallen condition than 'total depravity.' . . . *Radical* comes from the Latin word for 'root' or 'core.' Our problem with sin is that it is rooted in the core of our being" (148).

First, it refers to corruption at the very center of man's being, the heart, but this does not mean that man's humanity has ceased to exist. Second, it signifies the infection in every part of man's being, though this is not to infer that this infection is evenly distributed or that nothing good remains in man. Third, it denotes the total inability of sinful man to please God or come to him unless moved by grace, though this does not imply that man is not free in other areas of his life. Fourth, it includes the idea of the universal corruption of the human race, despite the fact that some peoples and cultures manifest this corruption much less than others.[17]

However, the point remains that sin has corrupted humans such that apart from the saving work of Jesus Christ, we are unable and unwilling to surrender to God and live as his servants. Thus, the first two great theological equalizers place humans in a unique tension: all humans are equally valued as beings made in his image, but also equally afflicted by sin; each human contains an identical value or worth, yet are trapped in the same spiritual condition: legally guilty and relationally alienated from God. So the old cliché remains true: "the ground is level at the foot of the cross."

One more point about sin: it has infected and warped creation, our only home. Scripture teaches God gave Adam and Eve authority over creation (Gen 1:28, "rule over") and instructed them "to work it and take care of it" (Gen 2:15). This implies nurture and development, not domination and destruction. Yet the fall of Adam and Eve led to the soil being "cursed" with "thorns and thistles" (Gen 3:17–18). The relationship between humans and the ecosystem, once harmonious and symbiotic, is now marked by alienation and abuse. Numerous agents—including individuals, cultures, and corporations—mistreat God's planet through unrelenting pollution of the air, soil, and water bodies, deforestation, overdevelopment, strip mining, poaching, overfishing, etc. This is why the Apostle Paul declares creation "has been groaning as in the pains of childbirth" (Rom 8:22). Why? The created order "was subjected to frustration . . . by the will of the one who subjected it, in hope that the creation itself will be liberated from its bondage to decay" (Rom 8:20–21). The relationship between the earth and its human inhabitants begs for reconciliation as well.

This complicated mess steers us toward the third great theological equalizer: God's atoning love.

---

17. Bloesch, *God, Authority, and Salvation*, 90.

The vast atoning love of Jesus Christ

By his grace, God's love covers human sin. Theologians call this the "atonement," which is "divine self-satisfaction through divine self-substitution."[18] The sacrifice of the sinless Son of God upon the cross removes our sin, purchases our pardon, and satisfies the holy justice of God. Through the atonement, sinners are given a new, regenerate nature through the indwelling Holy Spirit, clothed in the righteousness of Christ, declared to be innocent by God, the only holy Judge, and are subsequently adopted as children into God's family.

Theologians have long debated the nature and scope of the atonement: "While Calvinists have stressed limited or particular atonement, Arminians and Lutherans have emphasized the universality of the atonement."[19] I tend to agree with Donald Bloesch, who seeks to stake out a middle position:

> Those who emphasize the universal atonement of Christ are more faithful to the witness of Scripture, since we are told that God loved the whole world (John 3:16) and that Christ gave his life as a ransom for all (1 Tim. 2:6; cf. 1 John 2:2; Titus 2:11). Yet the Calvinists are right that the atonement not only makes salvation possible but also secures it, and in this sense it encompasses only those who respond in faith. Every human being is a blood-bought soul, as Wesley affirmed, but not all take advantage of their God-given opportunity. The truth in the doctrine of limited or definite atonement is that its efficacy does not extend to all persons. It is universal in its outreach and intention but particular in its efficacy.[20]

Ultimately, the atonement is about God's love. In John 3:16, the verb used for "love" ("*agapao*") refers to a love that is "deep-seated, thorough-going, intelligent, and purposeful, a love in which the entire personality (not only the emotions, but also the mind and the will) plays a prominent part, which is based on esteem for the object loved."[21] To this we can add the great lengths Rom 1–3 go to underscore the cross of Jesus is not intended for a particular ethnicity (and we could add sex, socioeconomic status, etc.) but for all humans. Indeed God is "rich in love" and so shares it with "all he has made" (Ps 145:8–9).

---

18. Stott, *The Cross of Christ*, 159.

19. Bloesch, *God, Authority, and Salvation*, 164.

20. Bloesch, *God, Authority, and Salvation*, 165.

21. William Hendriksen cited in Morris, *The Gospel According to John*, 769.

The final judgment

The Apostles' Creed states that Jesus Christ "shall come to judge the living and the dead."[22] The only holy and righteous God will judge *every single* human being by the same universally applied standards.[23] God does not mete out justice based on some whimsical sliding scale but according to "good or bad" (2 Cor 5:10) in his sight because "God does not show favoritism" (Rom 2:11). Jesus announced, however, that a definitive standard is how self-identifying Christians treated the "least of these" while on earth: the poor, marginalized, oppressed, and imprisoned (Matt 25:31–46). Those who have appropriated God's grace through Jesus Christ dispense it intentionally in grateful response to God's mercy and generosity.

To sum up the four great equalizers are the *imago Dei*, universal human sinfulness, the vast atoning love of Jesus Christ, and the inescapable final judgment. According to the Holy Scriptures, humans are equal in creation, equal in sinfulness, are equally loved, and equal in judgment. Although every society creates and enforces various hierarchies, assigning different people/groups various kinds of worth (depending on who has the power), ultimately, in God's sight, every human is equal.

Four postures

The four great equalizers will shape how reconcilers perceive and interact with others. Specifically, they animate four postures: certain attitudes that define the reconciling Christian. To begin, we are to approach all people with a posture of *profound humility*. More directly: each person you come in contact with is no more or no less worthy or valuable in God's sight than you are. He or she is God's image-bearer, afflicted with sin, offered Christ's atoning love, and will stand before the judgment seat of God. How then, for a second, could you or I entertain the falsity that "this person is less than me" or "better than me"? Humility leads to a clear sense of equality.

This reality calls for a second posture: *social inclusion*. Christians will approach and treat everyone as a potential friend—as one to be invited and included—rather than an enemy—one to be rejected and excluded. Put another way, reconciling affirms the significance of "embrace," which is "the will to give ourselves to others and 'welcome' them, to readjust our

22. Walt, *Creed*, xviii.

23. Rom 14:9-12.

identities to make space for them."[24] The Bible offers a specific word for embrace: hospitality. The Scriptures command Christians to offer hospitality to those inside and outside the faith.[25] The Apostle Peter indicates that love and hospitality are intertwined. After instructing Christians to "love each other deeply," the next verse adds, "Offer hospitality to one another without grumbling" (1 Pet 4:8–9).

What is hospitality? I am convinced it is often misconstrued. The running joke in the Hoffman house is my amazing, gifted-at-being-a-hostess wife frets far in advance, worries about dietary restrictions (an impossible minefield nowadays with everyone avoiding *at least* one of the following: gluten, dairy, sugar, non-alkaline water (?), non-ethically and/or non-locally sourced produce, etc. etc. . . .). She is an artist and a perfectionist and wants everything just so. I, on the other hand, do not sweat many (or any!) of the details and am more focused on giving my time and concentration. By the way, *both* the details and our full attentiveness are valuable and show love.

At its core, hospitality is creating space for another person and sharing your life and resources with this precious being. It involves a broad scope of activities: hosting her in your apartment or house, serving him/them by offering time, attentive listening, empathy, prayer, and perhaps financial gifts (1 Pet 4:10). Of course, hospitality involves reciprocity and thus includes receiving the gifts and caring gestures of the other person. To be clear hospitality does not necessarily imply a superficiality that avoids or glances over real differences, but rather engages the other with the respect and concern due a fellow human created in the triune God's image.

It should be said genuine hospitality will likely offend others. To dine with a person, in numerous cultures—past and present—is considered an endorsement of that person. That's why the Pharisees were appalled that Jesus would attend Levi's banquet, which reeked of scandal as it was chock full of "sinners"—social pariahs (Luke 5:27–32). Social convention meant any self-respecting rabbi would never sup with prostitutes or tax collectors, those traitorous Jews who colluded with the oppressive Roman government to steal and extort ("collect taxes") from their own kin and countrymen. But at times, being hospitable means following the Holy Spirit in overcoming some people's misunderstandings to welcome the other.

The third posture is *identification*. Look for existing bridges. Ask yourself, "What qualities, passions, and pursuits do I share with this person?

24. Volf, *Exclusion and Embrace*, 29.

25. Rom 12:13; 1 Pet 4:8–9.

What can we bond over? What is this person's story? And how might our stories overlap?"

Recently at my younger son's birthday party, I met two new people, both fathers. One was a stay-at-home dad who had been successful in the technology sector as a coder, but was now supporting his wife's rising career as a topnotch pastry chef. I quickly discovered he was from London, England, and had lived in Colorado. I shared about my three-year stint living in Denver and how I spent each June in Manchester, UK, during my PhD residency. (The commonalities ended there. Although we are both English Premier League (soccer) fans, he roots for Arsenal FC while I root for Liverpool FC . . . grr!!!) The other father described his pain undergoing an ugly and unwanted divorce. He was also very concerned about his children's use of technology, especially social media. I disclosed to him my parents divorced when I was young and that I too had great concerns about the ways the internet was molding my sons. Within minutes of meeting these strangers, we had surpassed pleasantries and plunged into deeper matters of the heart. Identification can spark meaningful connections.

The final posture is *mutuality*. This attitude dismantles all forms of superiority, separation, and defensive self-protection. You can learn something about God, the world, and even yourself from another person who is different. Every human carries wisdom and insight. "A broken clock is right twice a day" is true. Yet mutuality doesn't expect to gain anything. Rather, it is open to being surprised by the other, allowing for serendipity— unintended discovery leading to creativity and shared benefit. Mutuality is like jazz: multiple musicians playing different parts on different instruments can meld and harmonize to create something soaring, a piece that transcends independent solos.

The four great equalizers source four postures: humility, social inclusion, identification, and mutuality. Together, they form a vital reconciling substructure. Others will open their lives to us when they find us to be meek, hospitable, empathic, and genuinely interested in their personhood and passions.

Connecting the parts to the bigger picture: God's plan, God's people, and God's assignment

You have now been armed with four equalizers and four postures. But that's not enough. These resources must be integrated with God's plan, God's people, and God's assignment.

First is God's plan. Colossians 1 is significant for reconcilers because it articulates the character of Jesus Christ and breadth of God's mission:

> He [Christ] is the image of the invisible God, the firstborn over all creation. For by him all things were created. . . . For God was pleased to have all his fullness dwell in him [Christ], and through him to reconcile to himself all things, whether things on earth or things in heaven, by making peace through his blood, shed on the cross. Once you were alienated from God and were enemies in your minds because of your evil behavior. But now he has reconciled you by Christ's physical body through death to present you holy in his sight. . . . (Col 1:15–16b, 19–22b)

Five observations on this passage will give us insight into God's plan. First, notice how the Apostle Paul details the supremacy of Jesus Christ, who, because of his unrivaled power and glory, is the only person qualified to lead God's rescue mission.

Second, this passage beautifully encapsulates the relational narrative, presented earlier, of Creator-first creation-alienation-reconciliation-final creation. Colossians 1 indicates (a) the Trinity is eternal, predating creation ("the firstborn"); (b) God the Father created "all things" through Jesus Christ; (c) human alienation is due to sin (evil behavior); (d) our reconciliation is purchased by the cross ("his blood" and "physical body through death"); and (e) the process of sanctification ("to present you holy") which culminates in the final creation, the consummation of all things upon the arrival of the new heaven.

Third, the word "reconciliation" means radical change. The word Paul uses in Col 1:20 and 1:22 is *apokatallasso*, which translates "to reconcile completely" or "*to effect a thorough change back, reconcile.*"[26] The root word, *katallasso*,[27] means "to change (make other) or to exchange (provide an other). . . . The word was in use for the process of

26. J. H. Moulton and W. F. Howard cited in Morris, *The Apostolic Preaching of the Cross*, 215.

27. *Katallasso* is used six times in the New Testament: Rom 5:10 (twice); 1 Cor 7:11; 2 Cor 5:18, 19, and 20.

money-changing where one set of coins was exchanged for an equivalent set."[28] Reconciliation involves a dramatic change: when a person embraces Jesus Christ as Lord and Savior, she goes from enemy to friend, from guilty to innocent, from sinful to righteous, from criminal to (adopted) child, from the kingdom of darkness to the kingdom of light, from spiritually ignorant to spiritually enlightened, from death to life, from under wrath to under love, from broken to whole, from rejected to accepted, to name a few consequences. Reconciliation is a complete reorienting of God's relationship with humans and all of creation.

Fourth is the scope of reconciliation: "all things, whether things on earth or things in heaven." Reconciliation involves "making peace," which is the absolute healing and renewal of every centimeter of the cosmos, seen and unseen. More to the point, "making peace" is related to the Greek word *eirene*, which corresponds to the Hebrew word *shalom*. The word *shalom* is a soaring concept and so is difficult to translate into English. In the most simple of terms, it is life "characterized by love, equality and justice."[29] More broadly, it carries the idea of total flourishing, completeness, fullness, unity, peace, prosperity, and so forth. James Davison Hunter explains shalom this way: "a vision of order and harmony, fruitfulness and abundance, wholeness, beauty, joy, and well-being."[30] Shalom is the ultimate reality: "The end toward which the journey of reconciliation leads is the shalom of God's new creation—a future not yet fully realized, but holistic in its transformation of the personal, social and structural dimensions of life."[31] Reconciliation is all things, everywhere, experiencing shalom together.

Fifth, it bears repeating that God's plan to reconcile all things unto himself is radically countercultural and costly. Theologian John W. de Gruchy insists,

> In speaking of God in this way, Paul becomes the first Greek author to speak of the person offended as the one who initiates the act or process of reconciliation. This not only distinguishes Paul's use of the term 'reconciliation' from other Hellenistic sources, but also from other cultures and languages. For in the latter it is normally the case that reconciliation has to be initiated by the person responsible for the alienation and hostility, hence acknowledgement

---

28. Morris, *The Apostolic Preaching of the Cross*, 215.

29. Eric Law cited in Salter McNeil, *Roadmap to Reconciliation*, 120.

30. Hunter, *To Change the World*, 280.

31. Katongole and Rice, *Reconciling All Things*, 148.

of guilt becomes the precondition for reconciliation. But, for Paul, the gospel is precisely that God is the one who takes the initiative in seeking an end to hostility. Thus reconciliation in Pauline theology refers to the way in which the love of God in Jesus Christ turns enemies into friends thereby creating peace.[32]

This quotation highlights the stunning beauty of reconciliation: while humans sin against a holy God, it is that merciful God who initiates the rescue mission leading to the restoration of the broken relationship. The offended pursues the offender, not to retaliate, but to express love and heal the rift. God pays the cost of taking damaged goods (humanity and the entire cosmos) and making them new. This is a scandalous grace indeed.[33]

God's People

A key part of God's reconciling plan is the formation of God's people. Ephesians 2 sketches the contours of our new identity in Christ. Ephesians 2:1–9 states we are "saved by grace through faith." Salvation is God's free, unmerited gift to sinners. But it gets better! Verse 10 asserts God saved us so we could be his "workmanship, created in Christ Jesus to do good works which God prepared in advance for us to do." Workmanship is the Greek word "*poiema*" (where we get our modern word "poem" from) which is singular, and sometimes translated "masterpiece." Collectively, God's people are his masterpiece, created to do good works.

What are we supposed to do? In Eph 2:11–22, the Apostle Paul reminds his Gentile audience of their bleak condition before Jesus Christ came along. But now, Jesus Christ has "made the two one. . . . His purpose was to create in himself one new man out of the two"[34] different groups, Jews and Gentiles. The Church is God's most prized piece of art, the one that most showcases his reconciling plan and power. This occurred because the cross of Jesus "destroyed the barrier, the dividing wall of hostility" which is the Jewish "law with its commandments and regulations."[35] Jesus tore down

---

32. de Gruchy, *Reconciliation*, 52.

33. In his compelling book *Prodigal God*, Tim Keller explores the "parable of the Prodigal Son" (Luke 15:11–32) and demonstrates how the Father's love for his younger son is offensive to the "older brother" or "religious-moralistic types," including many who hail from "honor-shame" cultures.

34. Eph 2:14–15.

35. Eph 2:14–15.

the wall, the law, which kept the Gentiles out of God's kingdom. The essence of Paul's argument is that through the blood and cross of Christ, God reconciled or exchanged hostility for peace, division for unity, salvation by works for salvation by grace, the old humanity for the new humanity. The cross then, in its vertical and horizontal axes, represents both our new relationship with the triune God (the vertical axis) and our new, united relationship together (the horizontal axis). John Stott observes, "Christ crucified has thus brought into being nothing less than a new, united human race, united in itself and united to its creator."[36]

God's Assignment

Now that we have established God's plan and God's people, we arrive at God's assignment. The task of reconciliation is laid out for us in 2 Corinthians, considered to be one of the Apostle Paul's most autobiographical letters. In chapter 3, he depicts the glory of the new covenant in Christ. Then in chapter 4 he paints the portrait of Christians as "jars of clay": perishing bodies that contain the imperishable treasure of the gospel. In chapter 5, vv. 1–10, Paul describes how Christians "groan" and "long" to trade their "earthly tents" for their new, heavenly "dwelling." The Spirit is our "deposit, guaranteeing what is to come." Nevertheless, everyone must stand before the judgment seat of Christ and give account for how they used their earthly bodies.

With eternal life as the backdrop, 2 Cor 5:11–21 draws a captivating vision of reconciliation. Because of Christ's love, expressed most clearly in his death and resurrection, Christians are compelled to "regard no one from a worldly point of view" (v. 16). Why? "Because if anyone is in Christ, the new creation has come" (v. 17). While some translations use "creations," the word is singular in the Greek. The salvation God secured for us through Christ is profoundly social and interconnected. Yes, we are new creations as individuals, but God rescued and is purifying for himself his one and only "bride"[37] and "body."[38] This detail matters. It demonstrates reconciling is a communal posture and activity practiced by the entire body of Christ, and not reserved for the elite few, like pastors, missionaries, or social justice activists. No one is exempt. Why? God has reconciled us to himself through

36. Stott, *The Message of Ephesians*, 102.

37. Eph 5:25–26.

38. Eph 2:16.

Christ, thereby making us a new creation. And because "one died for all" we "no longer live" for ourselves "but for him who died."[39] If the heart of God is to reconcile all things unto himself, then this must become the heart of God's redeemed people, who are commanded to "as God's dearly loved children, be imitators of God."[40]

Consequently, Paul makes three bold declarations in vv. 18–20. The first is that God has given the body of Christ "the ministry of reconciliation" (v. 18). The word for "ministry" is the noun *diakonian*, which means "service, ministry, waiting tables." Most prominently, this word is found in Acts 6:1–7 where the apostles appoint *deacons* to distribute food to the widows in the early Church. Paul then uses a word that conveys the idea of practical care. Reconciling is concrete and holistic: it addresses the real, daily needs of people in direct, tangible ways. So it could involve making a cup of tea, helping a neighbor mow his/her lawn or grocery shopping, watching a person's pet while he goes on vacation, etc.

This kind of service is so vital to Christian witness, twice a year for many years our church did something called "Church Out": we cancelled both our Sunday morning gatherings and went out and served the community. This involved a wide range of activities: we picked up trash at the local park and beaches, we visited nursing homes and sang hymns, did crafts, and just loved on the residents, we fed breakfast to people facing food or housing insecurity, we baked brownies and cookies and gave them to the local fire and police departments, and we did basic cleaning and painting projects at local nonprofits. Most everyone we helped deeply appreciated our simple acts of kindness. The ministry of reconciliation often begins with small acts of service, done in love, and which convey genuine care for the whole person in her environment.

Paul's second pronouncement addresses evangelism: God has "committed to us the message of reconciliation" (v. 19). Genuine reconciling melds good deeds *and* good words. Verse 20 states God makes "his appeal through us. . . . Be reconciled to God." The word for "message" is the noun *logos*. It can be translated "a word, statement, or speech." *Logos* is the word employed in John 1:1–14: "in the beginning was the word" which refers to the pre-incarnate Jesus, and later on, "the word became flesh," referring to the incarnate Jesus Christ. Reconciliation is only possible because God the Father sent Jesus Christ, God's "word" or "message" to the world.

39. 2 Cor 5:14–15.
40. Eph 5:1.

Likewise, God calls all Christians to spread the "message of reconciliation": "Be reconciled to God." That is, by believing in, by trusting in the death of Jesus Christ, a person joins "the new creation" *and* becomes "the righteousness of God" (v. 21).

That's not all—it gets better! To drive home the primacy and efficacy of reconciliation Paul takes a third step. He moves beyond describing reconciling as a ministry and message, and asserts it is an *identity*: "We are therefore Christ's ambassadors" (v. 20). To understand reconciliation as a ministry and message is incomplete. It is more than a verb (serving and evangelizing) and a noun (the theological content of the gospel message). Christians are *ambassadors*. In the original language, this is a technical term employed only two times in the New Testament: 2 Cor 5:20 and Eph 6:20. The verb is *presbeuo*, which means to, "*be an ambassador or envoy*."[41] In many governments the president, king, or prime minister appoints an ambassador who is to represent his/her home country's best interests and the will of its leaders, in a foreign country. The ambassador is tasked with winsomely lobbying foreign leaders regarding his country's interests in various domains, such as immigration, trade, treaties, strategic partnerships, joint-military operations, etc. Make no mistake, an ambassador has to mediate between two countries who have conflicting needs, desires, pressures, and plans. As such, an ambassador must possess the skills and gravitas required to navigate between a host of competing agendas and clash of wills.

To illustrate: the United States' former Ambassador to Brazil, Peter Michael McKinley, in his "Farewell Message" recounted that during his tenure, the two countries "launched a bilateral security forum" in order to create "a strong mechanism for combating transnational and organized crime," "made it even easier for tourist and business travel by completing an Open Skies Agreement and opening a new consulate in Porto Alegre," and continued "the excellent cooperation we have developed to address infectious disease."[42] Not too shabby! It appears Ambassador McKinley was quite productive in representing the United States in Brazil.

Likewise, Christians, as "citizens of Heaven,"[43] represent and strive for God's reconciling purposes on earth in the unique places they inhabit. But because being a reconciler is an identity, and because it is the helix

---

41. Arndt et al., *Greek-English Lexicon*, 699.

42. U.S. Embassy & Consulates in Brazil, "Farewell Message by Ambassador McKinley."

43. Phil 3:20.

at the core of our spiritual DNA, we never resign our God-given mantle. At the moment of salvation, once a person is "born-again" or "born from above"[44] that person's citizenship, passport, and allegiance switch from creation (earth) to the new creation, where King Jesus is "making everything new"[45] and thus where God's shalom reigns: everyone and everything is healed, restored, and in right relations. Because that is our guaranteed future, reconciling is our present passion, imperative, and identity. Christ's ambassadors don't stop embodying and proclaiming the gospel of reconciliation until they are called home (death) or Christ returns at the consummation of all things. But this means we live in a perpetual tension. John Paul Lederach calls it "dreaming": "the simple act of connecting the present and the future."[46] We live by faith and order our lives "according to unseen realities."[47]

Two cautions

At this point, I must add two words of caution. First, the critics of reconciling have rightly asserted that oftentimes it takes the form of "making amends." I liken it to a forced parental intervention among siblings. When I was younger, my two sisters and I would clash over the use of a Star Wars toy, like Luke Skywalker's Speeder bike from the planet Endor. These kerfuffles could get heated, leading to hand-to-hand combat. (Thankfully, nobody had a real light saber!) Normally my parents handled it well and guided us to a fair resolution. But sometimes, instead of allowing us to work toward reconciliation, one of my parents took a more "assertive" or "proactive" role, inserted him or herself into the situation, and forced us, the aggrieved siblings, to "make up": "Paul, you tell Katie, 'I am sorry I stole the Speeder bike and hurt your feelings.'" "Now Katie you tell Paul, 'I am sorry I didn't share the Speeder bike . . .'"

But reconciling must not be reduced to soothing a family dustup. Reconciling is more than, "everybody stop fighting and get along right now!" For example, theologian Philip Sheldrake explains how true reconciliation differs from "political models of conflict resolution":

44. John 3:3. The Greek word is *anothen*, which is a play-on-words meaning "born again" or "from above."

45. Rev 21:5.

46. Lederach, *Reconcile*, 22.

47. Lederach, *Reconcile*, 25.

Several words are often treated incorrectly as interchangeable: reconciliation, conciliation, and accommodation. "Conciliation" is associated with pacifying or placating our neighbors from whom we are estranged. This lowers the temperature but does not necessarily promote deep change. For example, many local processes of conflict resolution aim to conciliate but fail to transform people at the deepest level. This leaves long-standing problems that will inevitably re-emerge in other guises. "Accommodation" or tolerance enables us to establish pragmatic arrangements, achieves a compromise but promotes a kind of parallelism. Here we learn to live alongside the "other" but avoid the kind of significant interchange that might mutually change us. Certain versions of multiculturalism in Western cities have faced this criticism. Pragmatic arrangements and compromise may initially be necessary in the world of *realpolitik*, but on their own they do not ultimately go far enough. Neither side needs to learn from the other or to be changed by the encounter.[48]

Hence, we must resist comprehending reconciliation in superficial ways: it is less a temporary ceasefire than a long-term armistice; less the end of the US Civil War (1860–1864) or World War II than Reconstruction and the Marshall Plan, respectively; less the mere election of Nelson Mandela than the Truth and Reconciliation Commission. We would do well to ponder the ruminations of Miroslav Volf, who observes "thin" or "zealous" Christian practice tends toward coercion, and so does not assist in genuine or generative reconciling.[49]

What is an example of "thin" reconciliation? Historian and ethicist Willie James Jennings, in reflecting upon America's history of failed attempts at racial reconciliation, utters this warning:

> I am convinced that before we theologians can interpret the depths of the divine action of reconciliation we must first articulate the profound deformities of Christian intimacy and identity in modernity. Until we do, all theological discussions of reconciliation will be exactly what they tend to be: (a) ideological tools for facilitating the negotiations of power; or (b) socially exhausted idealist claims masquerading as serious theological accounts. In truth, it is not all clear that most Christians are ready to imagine reconciliation.[50]

48. Sheldrake, *The Spiritual City*, 158–59.

49. Volf, *A Public Faith*, 39–43.

50. Jennings, *The Christian Imagination*, 9–10.

If I am interpreting Jennings correctly, he is critiquing the ways reconciling has been twisted by those in power. Meaning, instead of acknowledging, owning, and fully repenting of the sin of racism in our country's past, many white people have pressed to "move on," or "get over it." This sweeps our tragic history under the rug while attempting to gloss over an ugly blemish. But for many black people, the blemish is actually a persistently infected wound emitting pus, rather than a bygone scar. Instead, we must learn to face our failures with genuine contrition and cultivate a non-resentful re-membrance. It is to honor the fullness of memory, the ugliness, and loveli-ness, and everything in between.

To reconcile, we must ditch any insensitive attitudes, because they undermine the deep work of transformational learning at the heart of reconciling: empathic and embodied listening, methodical reflection, genuine repentance, an ardent commitment to relationship building, and systemic justice. To reconcile involves a reordering of spirit and flesh, rela-tionships and systems, hearts and laws. Brenda Salter McNeil reminds us, "Valuing reconciliation is *not* the same as actively engaging in a process that requires commitment and sacrifice."[51] I offer some inspiring examples in the next chapter.

My second caution is that we cannot guarantee the results of reconcil-ing. The consequences of our efforts are uncertain. Authors and practitio-ners Emmanuel Katangole and Chris Rice assert, "Reconciliation is not a theory, achievement, technique or event. It is a journey."[52] Indeed reconcil-ing is complex, messy, and a-linear. In practical terms, "its cultivation is often slow, laborious, and fraught with the thorns and thistles of discomfort and uncertainty."[53]

The upshot: to engage in reconciling means to enter a nebulous in-termediate zone, what philosophers call a state of *liminality*. Richard Rohr asserts, "We have to move out of 'business as usual' and remain on the 'threshold' (*limen*, in Latin) where we are betwixt and between. There, the old world is left behind, but we're not sure of the new one yet."[54] Theolo-gian Stuart Murray defines liminality as, "a transition between the familiar and the unknown, an unsettling process creating anxiety and vulnerability, where reluctance to abandon past securities jeopardises future prospects.

---

51. Salter McNeil, *Roadmap to Reconciliation*, 34.

52. Katangole and Rice, *Reconciling All Things*, 148.

53. Leong, *Race and Place*, 166.

54. Richard Rohr cited in Branch, *The Blue Book*, 191.

. . . Liminality offers opportunities for new discoveries and personal and communal maturing. But it feels threatening . . ."[55] Liminality feels like flying a two-seater Cessna plane enveloped by dark clouds while pummeled by thunder, lightning, and vicious cross-winds as you steer toward a novel location without knowing what that destination will look like or the coordinates to get there. You are confident you departed, but unclear as to the "where" and "when" of your arrival.

A particular story in Matt 14 provides an apt illustration. Jesus summons Peter to join him in walking on the raging waves of the Sea of Galilee. Peter becomes the first mortal on record to defy gravity and for a few seconds, tread upon H2O as if it were bedrock. Liminality is the interlude occurring when Peter climbed out of the boat and lasting until the instant Jesus clutched his panicked, sinking hand. Writer Jim Branch articulates its meaning: "It is the space *between*: between the boat and Jesus, between letting go and being taken hold of, between the old and familiar and the new and unknown, between control and agenda and dependence and detachment. . . . It is the space before your answer has come, or your problem has been solved."[56] Peter entered the danger zone, a portal thick with tension and uncertainty.

Let's pause for a gut check. Reconciling is both an arduous journey and a destination—albeit one that is not fully guaranteed on earth. Consequently reconciling should not be construed or pursued through the lenses of winning, conquering, succeeding, or the promise that applying specific formulas will ensure the desired results. From a human perspective, not every story concludes with a "happily ever after."

My messy story

I can personally testify to this bewildering truth. In my seventh year as the Lead Pastor of Evangelical Friends Church of Newport, I endured the scandal and heartache that comes from an ugly church split. To cut to the quick: because it is a torturous and convoluted story, and I do not have the space nor the wherewithal to describe it in full here, the Wikipedia synopsis will have to suffice.

Back in September of 2013, over a forty-eight-hour span, three staff members and one elder resigned their positions at our church. In rapid

55. Murray, *Post-Christendom*, 304.
56. Branch, *The Blue Book*, 190.

succession, the Spiritual Life Elder, Assimilation Pastor, Worship Pastor, and Youth Pastor all quit. I had barely returned from a ten-week sabbatical, and I felt like I had been church-jacked. Our denomination, the Evangelical Friends Church-Eastern Region, in consultation with our elder board, asked the four men to enter a reconciliation process with our church leaders (including me and our staff) led by a well-regarded outside reconciliation ministry. However, the four declined. Instead, a few weeks later they launched a "new" church two miles away and invited our parishoners to "like" it on Facebook. Long story short: we lost about 20 percent of the congregation, who migrated to the "new" church. Even worse, some people attended both churches for a while. Meanwhile, the reconciliation ministry commenced with its investigation and issued a gag order: no one at our church was to discuss the details of the conflict prior to the completion of a report to be presented at a congregational meeting. Time froze. That period was so painful, bewildering, and humiliating, I felt like I'd been swallowed by a suffocating black hole.

Thankfully, the reconciling ministry completed its inquiry and reported the results less than one month after the resignations. At the congregational meeting, I was left holding the bulk of the responsibility for the split. I confessed my contribution to the conflict and publicly repented for being prideful and impatient: that I had been more task-oriented than people-oriented, more hardheaded than empathic listener, and more impatient for results rather than trusting and waiting on God for his outcomes.

Today I see the debacle as a gift, a tender mercy from God. He pruned some ugly things from me (and hopefully, all of us). And I am convinced our church became healthier and stronger as a result. Indeed, as I began to reflect, heal, and recover, I dreamed that one day in the near future, all five of us would stand on a stage and announce that although we had sinned against our God, each other, and the hundreds of innocent people indirectly involved, that Jesus Christ had restored our shattered relationships and made peace. That yes, the gospel of reconciliation was alive and well in our midst!

Sadly, this vision has not come to pass seven years (and counting) after the split, even though all five of us live within a ten-mile radius of each other on a small island. The reality is complex and nuanced.

Ironically, the last of the four gentlemen to quit was the first to reconcile. Less than six months after his departure, he and his wife came to our house to meet with my wife and me. They repented of their sin, asked for forgiveness, and indicated a desire to reestablish our relationship. Today I delight in reporting he pastors a local church that is a strong partner with our church in leading initiatives that advance unity and reconciliation in the body of Christ through prayer. For this I praise God's goodness and grace.

The second man reconnected with me more than a year after the church split. We met at a café without our wives present and talked everything out, apologized, and cleared the air. We released all bitterness, frustration, and misunderstanding but were not sure exactly how to move forward given our busy lives. Although I've only bumped into him once or twice since our reunification (mostly due to positive changes in his life: welcoming a new daughter, moving houses, and a career change), he is an elder at the first man's church. As I understand it, they are doing significant ministry together—another win!

The third man and I are on affable terms. We have interacted numerous times and wave when we see each other. That process began a year after the split when he and his wife requested a meeting at the church. In all honesty, the appointment started out tense, even anguish-ridden. I was reminded our church was the first church they attended after becoming practicing Christians, they predated my wife and I as pillars of the church, and still live only a few hundred yards away. But both parties laid their cards on the table, took responsibility for their failings, asked for forgiveness, and put the past behind us. This good man is now a leader at another local church and has deployed the skills developed at our church to serve that congregation well.

Lastly, I feel sadness when I recall the fourth man, the main instigator of the conflict. Within two years of leaving and "planting" another church, he had some kind of falling out with his other three "friends" and "co-pastors." To my knowledge, he has yet to initiate reconciliation with them and denies any wrongdoing. Eventually, after the other three had departed, he closed the church, presumably due to a shortage of funds and parishioners. I've crossed his path a handful of times and it felt startling and awkward. Sometimes I waved and offered a feeble smile; other times I (in cowardice) pretended not to see him.

I remain disappointed by this outcome. I believe the gospel offers us so much more. But this is the liminality we must wrestle with as we seek to embody and declare the triune God's restoration of our flawed world.

The author of Hebrews was acquainted with the dense fog shrouding our deepest struggles and aspirations. Writing to a community facing antagonism for their Christian convictions, the writer exhorts them (and us) to "fix our eyes on Jesus, the author and perfecter of our faith, who for the joy set before him endured the cross, scorning its shame, and sat down at the right hand of the throne of God."[57]

Jesus, however, crossed the threshold of suffering, abandonment, and death for joy: the rapturous delight of reconnecting you and me with our Maker and returning the reconstituted cosmos back to its Creator-King. Jesus's actions inspire imitation. That is, as individuals and congregations, we can enter the stormy tumult, the space between the security of the boat and the surety of Jesus's grip to engage with people radically different, even hostile, to our faith. If Jesus endured the liminal space, we can too, right?

The promise of his presence

If so, it's only because Jesus promised his presence: "And surely I am with you always, to the very end of the age."[58] I've found the challenge is recognizing his presence.

My messy story comes with a twist. It was Sunday June 15, 2014, Father's Day, the day before my second son turned five, and approximately eight months after the church split. I was in Manchester, England, for my third PhD residency period (out of six). I chose to attend a pentecostal/charismatic church that met in a movie theatre nearby. My soul felt bruised and tender. The sermon was on Exod 14. After reading and explaining vv. 19–20, where the angel of God and the pillar of cloud shifted from the vanguard of Israel's army to their rearguard to protect them from the Egyptian army, the preacher stated, "Sometimes God works more behind us than in front of us." Those words struck a resounding note throughout the chamber of my heart.

Afterwards, during the closing time of worship in song, something astonishing occurred. A searing flash penetrated my consciousness, my holy imagination, and I saw Jesus encased in a radiant and warm light. He stood beside me with his right hand gently placed between my shoulder blades. I was instantaneously transported back to Thursday October 17, 2013. I stood before a packed sanctuary where I deliberately read a statement of confession and repentance. I remember feeling anxious and despondent as I alone took responsibility for the church split. But now, a calm balm gently

57. Heb 12:2.

58. Matt 28:20.

flooded over my spirit. Eight months later and thousands of miles away, this vision enabled me to peer through a supernatural lens and reinterpret that event. At the time, I perceived I was alone, but in reality, I had never been alone. Jesus was beside me, holding me up, consoling me during this darkest of hours. Then, the curtain closed.

After the service, I returned to my room on campus and inscribed this snippet in my journal: "Thank you Jesus for revealing your loving and comforting presence to me."

Conclusion

The substructure of reconciling theology is comprised of "the four great equalizers": the *imago Dei*, human sinfulness, the vast atoning love of Jesus Christ, and the final judgment. These doctrines will catalyze four postures: humility, social inclusion, identification, and mutuality. The postures are applied through God's plan, God's people, and God's assignment. That is, we are God's ambassadors who carry the message and ministry of reconciliation, which is nothing less than God's one, new humanity working for the total flourishing of the entire cosmos. We move forward both chastened and confident. On one hand we're aware of the ever-present temptation to settle for reductionistic forms of reconciliation. On the other hand, God's presence accompanies us.

With all this in mind, we arrive at the third fundamental section in the bridge: the superstructure of reconciling practices. Practically speaking, how can we best deploy our time, talent, and treasures toward reconciling? What might it look like in our communities? Are there examples and best practices we can glean from? To this we steer our gaze.

Questions for Reflection

1. Ponder the four "great equalizers" and four postures. Which ones do you agree with? Which ones do you find challenging to understand or apply in your own life? How might your city or town be different if more people adopted these ideas/postures?

2. Contemplate God's plan (to reconcile all things), God's people (one new humanity), and God's assignment (the message, ministry, and

identity [ambassador] of reconciliation). How are these ideas familiar to you? Are any of these concepts new to you, and if so, in what ways?

3. Have you ever been in a conflict where an outside party (parent or boss) intervened and imposed a "forced" peace? How did that make you feel? Did the conflict resolve itself or linger?

Practical Next Steps

1. Spend time in prayer asking the Holy Spirit to show you any prejudicial or superior attitudes you may possess toward an individual or group. Repent and ask God to change your heart.

2. Devote ten minutes a day for one week to reading aloud and studying 2 Cor 5:11–21. Then pray daily for the Holy Spirit to reveal to you a person or group of people in your life he would have you be Christ's ambassador to.

3. Rate yourself on a scale of one through ten: one is a low threshold for uncertainty (strong dislike of), and ten is a high threshold for uncertainty (accept it). Analyze your score. How does your past or personality influence your score?

4 The Superstructure: Reconciling Practices

EVERY BRIDGE HAS A superstructure. This refers to "the parts of the bridge that are mounted on top of the supporting substructure system . . . [including] everything placed above the main deck such as posts, steel truss system, bridge girder, cable-stayed system."[1] To review, the first two sections required to construct a reconciling bridge are the relational nature of the Trinity (the foundation) and a reconciling theology (the substructure). The final section is the superstructure of reconciling practices. Practices are habits and activities that promote reconciling across difference in each location we invest our lives. While this chapter offers illustrations and vignettes, these examples are intended to be more descriptive than prescriptive, more suggestive than instructive. Bridge building is highly personal and contextual: the gospel message is the same everywhere, but the way a Christian or congregation embodies and applies the Scriptures is contingent upon the leading of the sovereign, prevenient Spirit and the assets and liabilities of each community. In other words, each reconciler is to serve "God's purpose . . . in Christ as that purpose relates to *that* place."[2]

The onramp

Practices are crucial for multiple reasons. First, our behaviors shape and reinforce our desires, priorities, and worldview.[3] Second, our actions reveal the depth of our commitments: that is, "How do I know what I really believe until I see what I actually do?"[4] Although much more could be said, there are

1. See http://www.historyofbridges.com/facts-about-bridges/bridge-parts/.

2. Newbigin cited in Sunquist, *Understanding Christian Mission*, 153, emphasis original.

3. See Smith, *You Are What You Love*.

4. Cameron, *Resourcing Mission*, 1.

three vital habits I want to highlight: reconciling prayer, reconciling rhetoric, and forming reconciling communities and coalitions. These practices serve as the pavement Christians tread when bridging differences.

Reconciling prayer

"To clasp the hands in prayer is the beginning of an uprising against the disorder of the world," wrote Karl Barth.[5] Transformative and lasting reconciling can only occur when a church or community seeks the wisdom and empowerment of the Holy Spirit in prayer. Scott Sunquist correctly asserts,

> We must recognize the priority of spiritual labors (fasting, prayer, etc.) as opening the way for the Holy Spirit to work in mission. . . . Jesus's first command to the disciples in mission, in fact, was not to go and "do something" but to stay and wait for the Holy Spirit to come. Waiting is not passive, but is an active participation in the Spirit through prayer, fasting, and intentional silence.[6]

Prayer enables Christians to leave *chronos* or earthly time, and enter into *kairos* or eternal time governed by the Spirit.

So then, what does reconciling prayer look like? A few case studies that are local, regional, and international may prove helpful. Our church partners with four other area churches in a coalition called "One Church, One Prayer." The five congregations are diverse ethnically, denominationally, socioeconomically, and generationally. They gather on the first Monday of each month to worship and pray together. Each church takes turns hosting the meetings. A snapshot of these gatherings will reveal a sixty-something Afro-Caribbean lady from Dominica; a man dressed like he belongs to a biker gang with earrings, a shaved head, and tattooed arms; an immigrant teen girl from Central America; and a white middle-aged male in jeans and glasses (me?), singing with gusto and crying out in desperate prayer for ninety minutes. Our vision comes from Rev 7:9, where the Apostle John saw "a great multitude that no one could count, from every nation, tribe, people and language, standing before the throne and in front of the Lamb." John is granted a porthole into heaven—he observes what is currently and constantly occurring. First, Christians in heaven are not whitewashed like eggs in a carton. Apparently, they maintain their ethnicity: white, brown,

5. Barth cited in Fitch, *Faithful Presence*, 176.
6. Sunquist, *Understanding Christian Mission*, 239–40.

black, yellow, etc. Everyone, however, is reconciled: although different, they wear the same white robes (i.e., the righteousness of Jesus Christ) and worship God in harmony and unity. This reveals to me the deepest form of diversity within unity on planet earth is the body of Christ joining together to worship the ultimate Lamb that was slain.

What's more, Jesus taught his disciples to pray "your kingdom come, your will be done on earth as it is in heaven."[7] Jesus commands us to pray for God's will. What is God's will? That earth will conform to the reality of heaven. Heaven shows us the fullness and the completion of God's will. And it's the ultimate future for all Christians, a place of absolute love and thriving because it is devoid of sin, disobedience, pride, racism, classism, injustice, suffering, death, and evil. Now, if heaven is like this, if this is our destiny, and if Jesus taught us to pray "your will be done," then it stands to reason God would like us to pray that Rev 7 will become a greater reality here on earth. That's precisely why five churches from Newport County, Rhode Island, gather monthly to pray: so that although the Church on earth is oftentimes segregated by ethnic, age, sex, cultural, and class lines, God, through his Spirit, will break down these walls of division, and visibly restore and unite the body of Christ. We are asking for nothing less than God changing the spiritual, moral, social, and economic atmosphere in our region so it becomes more like the realest reality of all, heaven.

Specifically, at our monthly gatherings we engage in what author C. John Miller called "frontline" prayer by making three requests: "1. A request for grace to confess sins and to humble ourselves[,] 2. A compassion and zeal for the flourishing of the church and the reaching of the lost[,] 3. A yearning to know God, to see his face, to glimpse his glory."[8] Essentially, we ask God to cleanse us, to give us his eyes, and to reveal his heart. That's heaven, and we want to taste and reflect a tiny sliver of heaven in our place, our community, our home.

To be clear, One Church, One Prayer did not develop overnight. Many pastors and prayer leaders have contended for unity, reconciliation, and revival for decades. Along with my dear friend, mentor, and co-laborer, the Rev. Dr. Stephen Robinson, the black pastor of the multiethnic Crosspoint Church, and some other local pastors, we co-founded One Church, One Prayer in 2009. We started with seven churches gathering monthly. (It's not hyperbolic to say that's astonishing given our area contains around thirty-five

---

7. Matt 6:10.

8. C. John Miller cited in Keller, *Center Church*, 73.

Protestant churches!) But within two years, our coalition was fractured and limping, due to disagreements among the pastors over music style (contemporary vs. hymns), worship order (free-flowing vs. highly structured), and fears of competition and jealousy. This led to the dark years, the prayer famine of 2011–2013, when little unified prayer occurred.

Nevertheless, Steve and I kept contending for reconciliation. Thanks to the power of the Spirit, a renewal of sorts emerged from 2014–2018. As mentioned earlier, from 2014–2016 EFC Newport spearheaded The New England Festival of Hope. Simultaneously, Pastor Steve Robinson founded New England Prayerfest, a two-day prayer event held every October between 2014–2018. He enlisted my involvement and our church supported the event all five years through prayer, promotion, worship, financial, and logistical support. The goal was to unite the churches in the southeastern New England coastal region in order to pray for unity and reconciliation in the body of Christ, leading to revival. We prayed through the "Seven Mountains of Influence": Education, Arts/Entertainment, Government, Religion, Family, Media, and Business.[9] The first two years it was held in the Rhode Island Convention Center in Providence; the third year, held weeks before the 2016 election, took place at the Providence Performing Arts Center. The event was a potent demonstration of united prayer: how Christians of different ethnic, class, age, and denominational backgrounds could connect to seek a greater work of God in our region.[10] After much prayer and reflection, Steve discontinued Prayerfest to rest and pursue other opportunities.

In the end, all these prayer seeds began to sprout in 2018, when after a five-year hiatus, One Church, One Prayer restarted, with more unity and vigor than ever before. Apparently God is not done with Newport County, Rhode Island. A reconciling practice is leading toward a reconciled place.

But we are not alone. On a regional level is Together Advance the Gospel, formerly known as Love Rhode Island. This coalition, founded and led by Dr. Dave Gadoury, includes dozens of churches from greater Rhode Island and southern New England. The organization holds quarterly pastoral prayer meetings and annual prayer retreats or summits. The aim is "to reach people for Christ."[11] They recently initiated the "40 Days of Love" campaign, which involves praying for, caring for, and sharing the gospel with those in

---

9. Swanson and Williams, *To Transform a City*, 149–54.

10. For more information see Robinson, *Mega-Small Church*, 145–48.

11. "Together Advance the Gospel," https://www.togetheradvancethegospel.com.

our communities who might not have heard the good news about Jesus or don't identify as practicing Christians. Numerous people have discovered the love of Jesus Christ, or had their faith renewed through this dynamic campaign. Indeed the Holy Spirit is flowing throughout southeastern New England, reconciling people unto God and one another through unified prayer. We are witnessing lives being healed, new churches planted, and older congregations being revitalized. EFC has been honored to participate in Together prayer events and the 40 Days of Love.

Steve, Dave, and I have benefited from a wider prayer network I call the New York City Unity Movement,[12] built upon citywide prayer and collaboration among hundreds of churches, leading to "movement dynamics."[13] Tim Keller attributes the planting, growth, and prominence of Redeemer Presbyterian Church to dedicated prayer by two larger entities: his denomination, the Presbyterian Church in America, and the larger prayer movement already underway in the New York City region. In fact Mac Pier, Keller's friend, labels the prayer movement in the greater New York area, as *"the most significant urban prayer movement in the world."*[14] Pier's book *Spiritual Leadership in the Global City* describes the "New Urban Pentecost" taking place in New York City, as a collection of diverse organizations and congregations that have joined forces for spiritual and social renewal.[15] The emphasis on united and reconciling prayer has yielded tangible, even startling results: "In 1995, the murder rate in New York City peaked at more than 1,500 murders. . . . In the next five years, the murder rate would drop by 40 percent"[16] and that consequently, New York has recently become "the safest large city (of more than one million people) in America. God's people have been praying, and God has been answering."[17]

Lastly, reconciling prayer is happening on a global level. A fantastic example is the Jerusalem House of Prayer for All Nations, in Bethany, Mt.

---

12. I studied this movement as part of my doctoral research. It has been spearheaded by organizations such as Lead.NYC/Concerts of Prayer Greater New York, the New York City Leadership Center, Movement Day, Redeemer City to City, the Brooklyn Tabernacle (Pastor Jim Cymbala), and Christ Church, NJ (Dr. David Ireland), to name a few. See the website of Lead.NYC, https://lead.nyc/, or of New York City Leadership Center, https://movement.org/.

13. See Keller, *Center Church*, 337–77.

14. Pier and Sweeting, *The Power of a City at Prayer*, 21, emphasis original.

15. Pier, *Spiritual Leadership in the Global City*.

16. Pier, *Spiritual Leadership in the Global City*, 43.

17. As of 2002 (Pier and Sweeting, *The Power of a City at Prayer*, 34–35).

of Olives, Jerusalem. My brother-in-law, Tom Hess, founded this congregation—which he also calls "The Messianic Community of Reconciliation"—in 1987. Since then Tom has led continuous prayer (in the harp and bowl format of overlapping prayer and worship) from the roof of the House of Prayer. This congregation includes people from twenty nations. Every day, Christians pray in "Indonesian, Chinese, Hindi, French, German, Russian, English, Portuguese, Spanish, Turkish, Ethiopian, Hebrew and Aramaic!"[18] I have visited, worshipped, and participated in a two-hour prayer watch multiple times. It's a breathtaking experience that's hard to articulate. Additionally, Tom, and my sister Kate, host the annual All Nations Convocation, a two-week event which convenes thousands of prayer warriors, church planters, and government leaders from over 150 nations. Through this conference, and their relationships with other prayer networks spanning six continents, they are hearing stories of the Holy Spirit moving in miraculous ways across our diverse planet.[19] Movements rooted in prayer, unity, and reconciliation are fueling fresh spiritual awakenings leading to thousands of people embracing Jesus Christ as Lord and Savior.

While these stories provide some inspiration you may wonder: "What are some actionable steps that might assist me and my church family in pursuing reconciling prayer?" In response, I offer the mnemonic LIT: Lamenting, Interceding, and Transforming.[20]

Reconciling prayer involves lamenting the sin, brokenness, injustice, and divisions in our communities. Old Testament scholar Douglas Stuart contends that "more than sixty" of the 150 psalms in the Psalter can be classified as laments (a whopping 40 percent!).[21] Lament is so important there's a whole book of the Bible devoted to it: Lamentations. In his commentary on Lamentations, Professor Soong-Chan Rah writes,

> Laments are prayers of petition arising out of need. . . . Lament in the Bible is a liturgical response to the reality of suffering and engages God in the context of pain and trouble. The hope of lament

---

18. Hess, *Restoration of the Tabernacle*, 33.

19. In addition, they initiate quarterly pastor prayer summits that foster reconciliation among Messianic Jews, Arab Christians, and Gentile Christians doing ministry in Israel.

20. I confess my inspiration comes from my teen son Landon, who declares, "That's *LIT!*" to indicate his admiration. I hope he thinks, "That's *LIT!* I made it into Dad's book!"

21. Fee and Stuart, *How to Read the Bible*, 194.

is that God would respond to human suffering . . . [it] recognizes the struggles of life and cries out for justice against injustices.[22]

While lament holds a prominent place in the Bible, and as a reconciling practice, Rah is correct when he observes, "The American church avoids lament."[23] In my experience, white, evangelical churches tend to sidestep lament because it doesn't fit into the narrative of positivity, success, or growth that we often project. Lamenting contradicts the social media ethos of the "Instagrammable" life of fun, adventure, and coolness. Or because many white people have not personally experienced systemic injustice, we are ignorant of its damaging consequences. Lamenting prayer involves accessing and expressing complex and powerful emotions and so is neither neat, nor tidy, and thus does not fit comfortably into most high-energy, sixty-minute contemporary Protestant worship services.

However, cultivating lamenting prayer in our churches is crucial. Lament is the language of the soul for many brothers and sisters in Christ. Based on my limited study and experience of African American liturgy, lament, especially in the form of the "Negro spiritual" genre of songs, gave a voice to the millions of blacks, native Africans, and others, who endured a horrific existence under slavery.[24] Their pain is expressed through lamenting spirituals such as "Swing Low, Sweet Chariot," "Go Down, Moses," "Deep River," and "Balm in Gilead," to name a few.

How can we start to learn this new skill of lamenting prayer? I recommend pastors or Bible study group leaders do a study on the book of Lamentations or preach through a number of the psalms of lament to educate Christians on this practice. Second, it might be beneficial to set apart time in the worship services a few times a month to read a lament, and have a time of silent prayer or ask people to pray aloud, drawing from the language and emotions of the lament. Or perhaps try using a penitential prayer from *The Book of Common Prayer*.

Interceding is a second kind of reconciling prayer. In 1 Tim 2:1–2, the Apostle Paul "urges" his protégé Timothy "that petitions, prayers, intercession and thanksgiving be made for all people—for kings and all those in authority,

---

22. Rah, *Prophetic Lament*, 21, 23.

23. Rah, *Prophetic Lament*, 22.

24. Props to the late Prof. Anthony Campbell. I took his class "Preaching and Worship in the African American Traditions" at the Boston University School of Theology while in seminary. He had us read the classic book, *The Certain Sound of the Trumpet*, by Samuel D. Proctor, to better understand black preaching.

that we may live peaceful and quiet lives in all godliness and holiness." It is interesting to me that the Bible indicates our first posture toward our civic leaders is not one of unhinged ranting, pontificating, or saber rattling on social media, but prayer. We don't first talk to others about our politicians; we first talk to God. Interceding, then, is indispensible to reconciling.

The Greek word for intercession gives us insight into this practice. The word is *enteuxis*, which was a technical term denoting, "a petition . . . directed to a king."[25] Specifically, it meant to make a formal request before a king, similar to Esther's plea before King Xerxes.[26] The word also connotes the idea of a prayer that *"hits the mark,"* and subsequently brings about an *"intervention* led by God."[27] Intercessory prayer then, is approaching the King of all kings and making a specific appeal that he will intervene and deliver a particular outcome. Furthermore, Jesus taught we are not to ask with an attitude of groveling, but rather one of "shameless audacity."[28] A wise supplicant will not waste the king's time with a meandering, equivocating cup of drivel. No, she or he enters the king's presence because only the king has the power and glory required to deliver what is needed. Consequently, intercession calls for precision: it launches a smart bomb that aims for an exact target. So interceding prayer asks God to do things like:

- "Bring justice and equality to the racist and discriminatory structures (e.g., policing, courts, housing) like _____ in our region."

- "Remove the human traffickers from this zip code."

- "Help us bring an end to gun violence."

- "Tear down the ethnic tensions and prejudices between Hispanics, whites, Asian Americans, Native Americans, and blacks in our community."

- "Disband the gangs in our neighborhood through their leaders coming to a saving knowledge of Jesus Christ and/or through a mentoring ministry."

- "That corrupt city council member (insert name) be defeated at the polls."

25. Arndt et al., *Greek-English Lexicon*, 268.

26. Esth 5–7.

27. "1783. Enteuxis," emphasis original, https://biblehub.com/greek/1783.htm.

28. Luke 11:8.

- "Empower us to more proactively address drug addiction and mental health issues in our town/city."

- "That all forms of domestic violence will decrease in our county."

- "That the diverse churches in this region will cast aside their suspicions, distrust, and individual agendas and start expressing a kingdom-minded cooperation for God's glory."

- "Lead us to raise more resources for schools and nonprofits serving our community."

These are the kinds of audacious and specific prayer requests our King loves to answer.

The third letter in the mnemonic is transforming. To be clear, "The only enduring motive for prayer is that God is worthy to be sought."[29] Because God is lovely and majestic in and of himself, we seek him in prayer. The fruit of prayer, however, is transformation. The Bible is a compendium of stories of God answering the prayers of his people. Foremost, God transforms those who seek him in prayer, changing their hearts and perspectives. Yet those who pray are also conduits of God's grace and power, for we draw from and carry with us God's supernatural presence. But for transformation to occur, we must be attuned to God's movement in our midst: "The presence of God is the key that gives life and breath to everything we are trying to accomplish."[30]

This story may illustrate the potency of transforming prayer. Back in 2010, eight intrepid Christians from two churches in the Sacramento area obeyed the voice of God to start a new church in the Detroit Boulevard section of Sacramento. This neighborhood had a reputation due to its rampant "gang violence, prostitution, and drug arrests."[31] Nevertheless, these Christians remained undeterred because they relied on the power of prayer to reconcile and heal.

> [They] decided to walk through the neighborhood praying over each home and praying for the presence of Christ to reign over violence, addiction, and satanic oppression. One of the eight, Sacramento street detective Michael Xiong, reported that "each time we prayed over the houses, we felt the weight of oppression

29. Henderson, *Old Paths, New Power*, 224. Helpfully, he summarizes the Lord's Prayer as "He is worthy. We are needy" (126).

30. Robinson, *Mega-Small Church*, 144.

31. Fitch, *Faithful Presence*, 172.

becoming lighter." . . . [Soon after they] moved into the neighborhood and started what they called Detroit Life Church. A couple of years later the *Sacramento Bee* (the city's main newspaper) reported that there were no homicides, robberies, or sex crimes, only one assault, in Detroit Boulevard between 2013 and 2014.[32]

Christians must never underestimate the power of reconciling prayer: prayer that is Spirit-led, united, presence-centered, and involves genuine lamenting, interceding, and transformation.

Most vitally, prayer focuses our attention upward, which is where our reconciling help comes from. But the vertical gaze must eventually shift to the horizontal gaze: our outward-directed language.

Reconciling rhetoric

The second practice forming the reconciling superstructure is reconciling rhetoric. For many, the word "rhetoric" carries pejorative or negative connotations, akin to smarminess or manipulation. While I sympathize with that outlook, I do not share it. Rather, I agree with scholar James E. Beitler III, who defines it broadly as "the art of persuasion."[33] When it comes to Christian rhetoric, the thought of St. Augustine is foundational. He believed rhetoric "give[s] conviction to . . . truth"[34] and "Truth presented persuasively is sweet medicine."[35] For the Christian, the ultimate aim of rhetoric is "to help guide people into the joy and rest of the triune God."[36] Simply put, righteous rhetoric leads humans into a relationship with their Creator.

This is why the Holy Scriptures indicate our words have real power: to bless or curse, to heal or destroy.[37] "Do not let any unwholesome talk come out of your mouths, but only what is helpful for building others up according to their needs, that it may benefit those who listen," commands the

---

32. Fitch, *Faithful Presence.*

33. Beitler, *Seasoned Speech*, 2.

34. Cited in Beitler, *Seasoned Speech.*

35. Beitler summarizing Augustine's thought in *On Christian Teaching*; Beitler, *Seasoned Speech*, 3.

36. Beitler summarizing Augustine's thought in *On Christian Teaching*; Beitler, *Seasoned Speech*, 2.

37. A small sample includes dozens of verses in Prov 10–31; Jas 3; the teachings of Jesus, etc.

Apostle Paul.[38] Language is far more than breath, vocal chord movements, and sounds emanating from a mouth. Our speech can define perception and identity. Rhetoric scholars term this the "constitutive function" of language, which means, "the identities of both rhetor [speaker] and audience are fashioned in and through the language we use. The language we use not only *references* but also *shapes* reality."[39] Our speech, due to its limitations, trades in addition and subtraction and thus inclusion and exclusion: "Even if any given terminology is a *reflection* of reality, by its very nature as a terminology it must be a *selection* of reality; and to this extent it must function also as a *deflection* of reality . . . any nomenclature necessarily directs the attention into some channels rather than others."[40]

The Apostle James provides the first principle of righteous rhetoric: "Everyone should be quick to listen, slow to speak and slow to become angry."[41] As a minister (one who is somehow miraculously compensated to speak often!) every time I read or hear this verse, my spirit cries "ouch" with holy conviction. To my shame, I have failed many times to heed James's warning. And then I cry "double ouch" when I consider the example of my Savior, who "was oppressed and afflicted, *yet he did not open his mouth*; he was led like a lamb to the slaughter, and as a sheep before its shearers is silent, so *he did not open his mouth*."[42] Thus as God's bridge builders who work across the chasms of conflict, our first posture should be one of silence and listening.

I believe this is especially true given Christians have earned a reputation in many circles for being garrulous hacks and judgmental windbags due to our over-involvement with partisan politics and social media. Consequently, James Davis Hunter makes this recommendation:

> It is not likely to happen, but *it may be that the healthiest course of action for Christians . . . is to be silent for a season and learn how to enact their faith in public through acts of shalom rather than to try again to represent it publicly through law, policy, and political mobilization.*

---

38. Eph 4:29. The word "unwholesome," in the original language means "putrid, rotting." What a graphic image! Speaking negatively is like spewing vomit upon a person.

39. Beitler drawing from Kenneth Burke; Beitler, *Seasoned Speech*, 136, emphasis original.

40. Kenneth Burke cited in Beitler, *Seasoned Speech*, 136–37, emphasis original.

41. Jas 1:19.

42. Isa 53:7, emphasis mine. Remarkably, the Gospels underscore Jesus's silence. See Matt 27:14 and John 19:8–10.

This would not mean civic privatism but rather a season to learn how to engage the world in public differently and better.[43]

This is something to consider. It also echoes the proverb, "Even fools are thought wise if they keep silent, and discerning if they hold their tongues."[44] Similarly, the cheeky truism—often attributed to Mark Twain or Abraham Lincoln—states, "Better to remain silent and be thought a fool than to speak out and remove all doubt." An endless gush of words dilutes their clout. Reconcilers will prioritize silence and active listening because they are dynamic forms of communication that convey humility and genuine care.

Next, besides listening, reconcilers will—at all costs—avoid lobbing rhetorical firebombs and firmly but gently rebuke those who do. John Inazu, in his excellent book *Confident Pluralism*, warns against "two particularly destructive forms of speech: the hurtful insult and the conversation stopper."[45] Bullies use hurtful insults such as *"fat, ugly, stupid, friendless"* to "wound" their victims or will even deploy put-downs based on a person's race or sexuality, like "you're so gay."[46] This kind of language is destructive because it attempts character assassination. To attack another person in this way is despicable and unacceptable. Inazu explains why the hurtful insult is so pernicious: first, it "is almost impossible to regulate under the First Amendment;" and second, it "is *socially constructed*. It gains force and power by the cultural context that surrounds it."[47] Unfortunately, slurs cannot be readily curbed or punished by the US legal system. And generally speaking, unless someone has adequate financial resources, it is challenging to seek restitution through the civil courts, i.e., filing charges for slander or defamation of character.

The second rhetorical firebomb to avoid is "the conversation stopper." In that case the aggressor spews charged epithets like *"close-minded, extremist, heretical,* and *militant* . . . 'Baby Killer' and 'phobic'"[48] which intends to make "debate irrelevant and frequently impossible."[49] According to Inazu, one egregious example is "bigot":

43. Hunter, *To Change the World*, 281, emphasis original.
44. Prov 17:28.
45. Inazu, *Confident Pluralism*, 96.
46. Inazu, *Confident Pluralism*, 97–98, emphasis original.
47. Inazu, *Confident Pluralism*, 97, emphasis original.
48. Inazu, *Confident Pluralism*, 98–100, emphasis original.
49. Inazu, *Confident Pluralism*, 98.

[Which] frequently appears against religious believers and groups that maintain traditional beliefs about sexuality in their internal membership requirements. . . . To be sure, some religious believers *are* bigots: they "strongly and unfairly dislike other people" and treat others with "hatred and intolerance." But the bigotry label is not generalizable to all religious believers who hold traditional beliefs about human sexuality, even when those beliefs lead to "discrimination" by private groups . . . [this pejorative term] attributes a particular motive to an action. And it does so with rhetorical force. We can debate whether some acts of discrimination are good or bad or simply neutral (like discriminating between two wines). But there are no good bigots. Some of the people using the *bigot* label think that is exactly the point: there are no good bigots. From their perspective, *every* act of exclusion of gays and lesbians is a bigoted act, and therefore the label is morally appropriate.[50]

On the other hand, people of faith will be wise to grasp that "not all disrespectful words and not all political decisions that disadvantage believers will rise to the level of persecution. Jumping too quickly to unwarranted defensive language can also wall off relationships and end dialogue."[51] In all its permutations, these kinds of reactionary discourse are more destructive than constructive, more antagonistic than engaging, more corrosive than life-giving.

In short, reconcilers are called to abide by a higher standard than what is permissible under the US Bill of Rights and First Amendment. Bridge-builders and peacemakers assent to Jesus's teaching that those who use contemptuous or debasing language will incur God's judgment.[52] We find a salient cautionary tale in Num 20, where Moses directly disobeys God's orders, strikes a rock in anger, and calls the Israelites a derogatory term. In an instant, the reward of decades of faithful leadership (entering the promised land) is taken from him. The consequences of the hurtful insult and conversation stopper are to be taken seriously.

The third part of reconciling rhetoric may be the most crucial one. But before I plunge in, I want to make an important distinction. There exists at least two kinds of rhetoric: internal rhetoric (insider directed) and external rhetoric (outsider directed). Internal rhetoric can be understood as private conversations inside the Church or local congregation. In this case, Christians

50. Inazu, *Confident Pluralism*, 98–99, emphasis original.

51. Inazu, *Confident Pluralism*, 98.

52. See Matt 5:21–24.

are expected to teach and uphold the orthodox Christian faith[53] and that of their particular denomination/tradition/polity.[54] In other words, their focus is on fidelity to the Scriptures and their denomination or history.

With that in mind, I want to suggest a different approach regarding external, or outward facing, rhetoric. It is animated by Col 4:5–6: "Be wise in the way you act toward outsiders; make the most of every opportunity. Let your conversation be always full of grace, seasoned with salt." Following this admonition, reconciling rhetoric will be a genuinely *repentant* rhetoric. Beitler, reflecting on the sinfulness and brokenness both inside and outside the Church, argues,

> Our witness must involve acts of private and public repentance— our own turnings—alongside our call to others to repentance. In fact, the power of our witness may ultimately rest not in our ability to convince others of their need for repentance but in our willing- ness to make ourselves vulnerable to others by confessing to—and actively seeking to redress—the injustices we have perpetuated.[55]

But repentance is more than just a public action. It comes from a deeper place. Scholar Jennifer McBride offers a theology of public witness called a "mode of being in the world [that] is confession of sin unto repen- tant action."[56] This means Christians, when speaking to the broader public (in a format that inhibits direct, face-to-face interaction, whether on social media, TV, blogs, podcasts, etc.), will demonstrate humility "through an overlapping confession of their own sin and the sin of broader society."[57] McBride places flesh on these bones:

> By "confession of sin" I mean more broadly a pattern of speaking characterized by humble acknowledgement of complicity in spe- cific sin and injustice and of the church's inherent interconnect- edness in the sin of broader society. . . . By "repentance" I mean the church's concrete activity in social and political life that arises

---

53. In my opinion, that is the essential Christian doctrines outlined in the Apostles' and Nicene Creeds.

54. This includes ecclesiology, the ordinances, views of marriage, sex, war, money, etc.

55. Beitler, *Seasoned Speech*, 156. By his own admission, Beitler is influenced by Jen- nifer McBride. She, in turn, is influenced by the works of Dietrich Bonhoeffer.

56. McBride, *Church for the World*, 11. For McBride, "mode of being" is an ongoing disposition, attitude, or posture.

57. McBride, *Church for the World*, 6.

from accepting its responsibility and acknowledging its complicity in such sin.[58]

We may read the above paragraph and wonder, "Why would I repent for other people's sins?" If so, you are not alone. Many people in Western, late-modern societies tend to be highly individualistic. We think and move through life using "I" more than "we": i.e., "how will this choice reflect on me?" versus "how will this choice reflect on my family (or ancestors, company, church, etc.)?" Because so many people wrestle to comprehend how interconnected human beings are, they cannot understand the idea of social/corporate culpability for sin. However, the reality of history is that regarding social/familial/national sins, everyone is complicit and can oftentimes occupy multiple roles simultaneously, including victim, perpetrator, and beneficiary.[59]

Thankfully, our interconnectedness also works to our benefit. In fact the gospel is predicated upon the interrelated notions of identification, vicarious substitution, and federal headship. The Apostle Paul expounds upon these ideas in Rom 5: "Sin entered the world through one man [Adam] . . . in this way death came to all people, because all sinned. . . . [But] how much more did God's grace and the gift that came by the grace of the one man, Jesus Christ, overflow to the many!"[60] John Stott clarifies the phrase "all sinned": "There can be only one explanation. All died because all sinned in and through Adam, the representative or federal head of the human race."[61] Yet Jesus Christ is the "new Adam," the far greater and more glorious federal representative, the vicarious substitution, who bears our sins in his body, dies in our place, and grants us forgiveness, justification, a new nature and identity in his name. By extension, it follows that Christians can represent the saving work of Jesus Christ by humbly repenting of the collective sins of society. This is an act of truth (Christians who are being sanctified still battle some lingering sins and are part of society), identification, and solidarity.

What's more, we would benefit from pondering other examples of vicarious or representative repentance in the Scriptures, including those found in Ezra 9 and Neh 1. In Ezra 9, the Israelites "confessed their sins and

---

58. McBride, *Church for the World*, 17.

59. See Beitler, *Seasoned Speech*, 128–60. The illustration is apartheid in South Africa.

60. Rom 5:12, 15.

61. Stott, *The Message of Romans*, 152.

the wickedness of their fathers."[62] When Nehemiah hears the terrible news of Jerusalem's ruined condition, he spends days mourning, weeping, and fasting before he finally prays, "I confess the sins we Israelites, including myself and my father's house, have committed against you. We have acted very wickedly toward you."[63]

The witness of Jesus, Ezra, and Nehemiah challenge the strident rhetoric numerous Christians in the US have oftentimes displayed in recent years. Specifically, McBride points to "the tendency to identify witness with possession of truth and the tendency to presume that Christians are called in public life to be the standard-bearers of morality."[64] Whether intended to or not, this commonly gives the impression that Christians are smug or triumphalist, which is problematic on multiple fronts. Why? Reasons abound: Christians sin and fail,[65] Jesus commanded his followers to acknowledge and confess their sins before they accuse others of sin,[66] Christians are to imitate the humility of Jesus Christ and "do everything without complaining or arguing,"[67] judgment starts in the Church,[68] and that the only all-knowing and sinless judge of hearts and behavior is God.[69] The priority of Christians, now and always, is to pick up their crosses daily and follow Jesus[70] and to love their enemies and pray for those who persecute them.[71]

So then, how can we express reconciling rhetoric to the wider public? Here are some suggestions:

- Whenever possible, rather than oppositional language ("us" vs. "them"), use inclusive language. For example, "We, the Christian community in this city/state/region/country, have sinned and disobeyed your commands as it relates to _____. Although we are a small part of this wider city/state/region/country, we do not cast any blame nor make any excuses. We have been a poor witness. And

62. Ezra 9:1–37.

63. Neh 1:6–7.

64. McBride, *Church for the World*, 17.

65. See Rom 7; 1 John 1; etc.

66. Matt 7.

67. Phil 2:1–18. Although this text pertains first to those inside the Church, it also applies to our relations outside the Church as well.

68. 1 Pet 4:17.

69. Matt 13:24–30, the parable of the weeds or tares.

70. Luke 9.

71. Matt 5:43–48.

because human beings are profoundly interconnected, we repent. On behalf of all those in this area who have failed as we have, we ask you, O God, to forgive us, cleanse us, and grant us the desire to do right going forward."

- Employ specific language when confessing: "we have neglected the needs of the poor, including housing, etc." "We have abused the earth you gave us to care for," "We have worshipped the idol of _____," etc.

- Use scriptural language and include references as often as possible: "The Holy Scriptures teach us in 1 Cor 6 that sexual immorality is a sin because our bodies are temples of the Holy Spirit," or, "The Holy Scriptures teach in Prov 14:31 that 'whoever oppresses the poor shows contempt for their Maker,'" etc.

- It may prove helpful to read lectionary prayers of confession, e.g., *The Book of Common Prayer* or recite a psalm of lament.

It is my firm opinion that Christians use this kind of language for the vast majority of our public declarations: whether on social media, YouTube, podcasts, etc. There are exceptions, however. Obviously a sermon from a worship service is primarily speaking to insiders. Yet if a preacher or teacher knows that the sermon or talk will be recorded and disseminated widely, I urge that person to be cautious and measured in their language and tone, e.g., "it is the Christian understanding, based on 1 Cor 6, that sexual sin is defined as _____."

Another exception is when a peacemaker or reconciler is invited to give a Christian perspective in a public debate or forum. When quoting Scripture it might be good to say, "As I understand the meaning of— TEXT—, it states _____." In addition, I recommend you consider whether it is profitable to participate in a public debate or forum that does not allow for proper follow-up or clarification. If it is placed on Facebook or YouTube, will you, the Christian speaker, have the ability to respond to comments or questions? If not, there may not be an adequate opportunity for a gracious dialogue, which could be unhelpful for all involved.

In the final analysis, I believe it is best for Christians to start with deep silence and listening when entering a conversation. When words are called for, we will use reconciling rhetoric, which stresses humility, confession, and repentance. Because words are powerful, because our communities are polarized, because the Church has failed countlessly, and because only

Jesus Christ is the sinless judge, bridge-builders will carefully guard all the ways they communicate—in words, tone, attitude, and body language.

Forming reconciling communities and coalitions

The third habit presented here is the forming of reconciling communities and coalitions. Reconciling is not a solo sport—Christians can only serve as reconcilers when in relating regularly with others. As my friend Stephen Robinson reminds me often, "we are better together!" But that means the gathering of affiliated groups around shared goals and causes is perhaps the most gut-wrenching, soul-testing, and time-intensive part of reconciling. So many factors make coalition building complex and messy: (1) the spiritual condition and needs of each unique place; (2) the nature of relationships among local churches and Christians; (3) a person or church's theological background/polity/tradition, including their view of political engagement;[72] and (4) the work of the Holy Spirit in that place. All of these variables make it undesirable and unrealistic for me to prescribe "the ideal model" or offer a set of "iron-clad, guaranteed-to-work principles/methods."

With that said, on the other hand, it's worthwhile to state some values that contribute to the formation of reconciling communities and coalitions. Let's start with the overarching goal: to move closer to embodying Rev 7 in our neighborhoods. Martin Luther King Jr. captured its essence when he painted the vision of "The Beloved Community": "the new social space of reconciliation" created by "the great *event* [calvary] that stands at the center which *reveals* to us that God is on the side of truth and love and justice."[73] When the Beloved Community (or reconciling coalition) holds a steady gaze at the sacrificial and healing love of Jesus Christ for all creation, God grants them the ability to nurture *shalom*, the flourishing of truth and justice among a mosaic of people. This occurs most powerfully when we are intentionally connected to the mutual life of the triune God, which binds us together in compassion and faithfulness.

The first value is a commitment to *prayerful and communal discernment*. This involves a medley of individuals and leaders, congregations

---

72. For example, Amy Black, a professor of political science, maintains there are five major Christian perspectives regarding partisan politics: "The Anabaptist (Separatist) View, the Lutheran (Paradoxical) View, the Black Church (Prophetic) View, the Reformed (Transformationist) View, and the Catholic (Synthetic) View." See Black, *Five Views*.

73. Cited in Marsh, *The Beloved Community*, 50.

and organizations, gathering in God's presence to collectively listen to the voice of God. This activity brings "a discernment of the working of the Spirit and of the Antichrist"[74] in our community. So then, reconcilers will pose these kinds of questions: where is God moving in our community? Where is the devil (evil) operating in our community? Where are the areas of pain and despair? What are the bright spots? Who is taking initiative and having success? Exploring these issues will lead a group to decide what they are working for and/or what they are working against. For instance, "we are for ethnic reconciliation in the face of prejudice" or "we are for safe and healthy homes in the face of child abuse and neglect," and so on. One way to start is to engage in prayer walking or what prayer researcher George Otis Jr. calls "spiritual mapping."[75] Another option is to prayerfully perceive "a story of self, a story of us and a story for now."[76] This would involve drawing a Venn diagram that includes individual stories in that place, the community's history and most pressing needs, and the reconciling Spirit's mission, in the here and now.

A second value is *the primacy of locality*. Although the prominence of place was highlighted earlier, I want to underscore it again due to the unprecedented and unrelenting rise of partisanship identity and the nationalization of our politics. Reconcilers must not allow national issues to override or displace local ones. Catholic social teaching uses the term "subsidiarity": "This principle argues that it is wrong to assign to a greater or higher association what a lesser or smaller association can do for themselves."[77] Following this line of thinking, theologian Alan Roxburgh poses this provocative question: "What might social, political and economic life look like if Christians began with the conviction that in God's kingdom it is in the local, in the *commons* that the new creation begins to be birthed and discerned?"[78] This means each congregation or partnership a) dedicates itself to investing in and caring for its city block or neighborhood, and b) refuses to interfere with local autonomy and stewardship, and in doing so, encourages residents and citizens (the "boots on the ground") to continue engaging and fulfilling their responsibilities.

74. Oliver O'Donovan quoted in Bretherton, *Christianity and Contemporary Politics*, 56.

75. See Otis Jr., *Informed Intercession*.

76. Taylor, *Mobilizing Hope*, 26.

77. Roxburgh, "Reclaiming the Commons," 6.

78. Roxburgh, "Reclaiming the Commons," 6.

The third and final value is a centered-set approach.[79] On one hand, a bounded-set approach to coalitions defines "who's 'in' our group" and "who's 'outside' our group";[80] a centered-set approach unites distinct, and even opposing groups together around a shared goal (e.g., reducing abortions—see example below). For instance, the "Unite to Pray Against Hatred" rally I organized (see Conclusion) was a centered-set event: it included Christians from various traditions, and even some people who did not appear to identify as Christians (I don't mean to be ungracious but when one person prayed, it was not clear to me what religious convictions were being expressed. However, I remain thankful for that individual's participation!). In other words, a centered-set approach has minimal criteria for participation whereas a bounded-set approach has strict standards based on clearly defined "insiders" and "outsiders." So at the rally, I allowed a female minister to help lead the crowd pray through Matt 5, even though I am pretty sure we disagree on some theological points.[81]

That brings us to some illustrations. It bears repeating these reconciling entities are more illustrative than prescribed—they are intended to serve as concrete examples of what best practices look like, rather than models to be cloned. I am presenting two categories here: 1) new communities (which are generative bodies) and 2) coalitions (partnerships among diverse groups that choose to associate together).

New communities are birthed from scratch to embody and reflect the reconciling mission of the Trinity in our world.

- **Voice of Calvary Ministries:** started by John Perkins and located in Jackson, Mississippi. This ministry is premised upon the "Three Rs of Christian community development—relocation, reconciliation, and redistribution."[82] Perkins pursues a holistic approach to urban

79. For more information, see Keller, *Center Church*, 291–336.

80. One example is church membership. In most cases, any person, whatever his/her beliefs, is free to join us for worship on Sundays or other programs. However, church members sign a covenant agreeing to uphold certain theological tenets and behaviors. We also have regular attendees, who participate in our community but have not officially joined. When we hold a congregational meeting, while both groups are invited, only members can vote.

81. Here I am thinking about human sexuality and the authority of the Scriptures. Incidentally, about ten months after this rally, one of our church's ministry leaders expressed anger at my centered-set approach, quit his post, and left our church. I was shocked by his vehemence—I had never seen him display an expression of deep emotion.

82. Perkins, *With Justice for All*, 13.

ministry, one that addresses the complexities of poverty, race, and locale. The organization includes a church, thrift store, gymnasium/community center, preschool, and legal services. The aim is to nurture the flourishing of blacks, whites, Hispanics, and others in that region.[83]

- **New Song Community Church:** located in the Sandtown neighborhood of Baltimore, Maryland. Mark Gornik and Allan Tibbles, a quadriplegic, founded the church. The congregation, following the lessons of John Perkins, seeks to foster reconciliation and shalom through renovating old houses (more than two hundred!), creating affordable housing, starting a preschool learning center and academy (middle school), a health center, an employment center, and promoting the arts through a children's choir.[84]

- **NewSong Church:** Dave Gibbons founded this church in Irvine, California, in 1994. As a biracial man (white and Korean), he had a "vision of multi-ethnicity and ethnic reconciliation and reaching the next generation."[85] However, about a decade into pastoring the church, he became dissatisfied leading a megachurch, and in particular, one driven by church-growth methods and metrics, and the task of raising millions of dollars to construct a massive church facility. He asked himself, "Am I just building a bigger shoebox for people to sit and listen and leave? Do I want to raise all this money for a bigger shoebox?"[86] Consequently, he moved his family to Bangkok, Thailand, for a year. His time of living in another culture inspired Dave to make profound changes upon returning to California. Dave scuttled NewSong's building campaign and moved the church to Santa Ana, a less-affluent community with greater material needs. NewSong started shifting its focus toward planting "verges": "organic-sized churches" of thirty to three hundred people that emphasize decentralized, local leadership and being flexible, contextual, and creative in their outreach.[87] The church

---

83. Perkins, *With Justice for All*, 131–44. For more info go to Voice of Calvary Ministries' website, http://vocm.org/.

84. Gornik, *To Live in Peace*, 163–95. For more info go to New Song's website, https://www.nscommunity.org/.

85. Gibbons, *The Monkey and the Fish*, 207.

86. Gibbons, *The Monkey and the Fish*, 208.

87. Gibbons, *The Monkey and the Fish*, 206–11. The book defines its approach as "fluid" and "third-culture." Also see NewSong's and Verge Network's websites, http://

planted new verges in places like Skid Row in Los Angeles, Mexico City, London, and Bangkok. These groups gather in various settings like pubs in London and clubs in Bangkok and build relationships with people wrestling with drug addiction and poverty, the creative/artistic communities, sex-trafficking victims, and young singles.

- **Crosspoint Church:** started by Pastors Stephen and Mary Robinson in 1999 to be "a house of prayer for all nations." It is a multiracial, cultural, and generational congregation focused on promoting reconciliation through discipleship and prayer. They have a strong mentoring presence in the Florence Gray Community Center in the northern end of Newport, Rhode Island, which faces poverty and broken homes.[88]

These four congregations exemplify a reconciling DNA: embedded in their understanding of the gospel is the active pursuit of building bridges across barriers, including ethnicity, class, age, sex, etc.

The second category is reconciling coalitions or partnerships. These are comprised of congregations and other groups/organizations that retain their identities, but strategically collaborate with others in pursuit of reconciliation and unity.

- **Evangelical Friends Church of Newport:** the congregation I have had the honor of serving has started initiatives like the New England Festival of Hope, and One Church, One Prayer Newport County. EFC Newport has collaborated with outside groups like New England Prayerfest, Together Advance the Gospel, and the Newport Partnership for Families.[89] This includes donating financial resources, volunteer hours, promotional and logistical help, and prayer support. The locus of investment is efforts that promote reconciliation and flourishing in our region through prayer, cross-denominational unity, interracial dialogue, and support for families and marginalized groups. One inspiring example was the "The Year of Care" campaign in 2017. Over twelve months, EFC partnered with five agencies we had existing relationships with (two were explicitly Christian and three were

---

newsong.net/ and https://www.vergenetwork.org/.

88. Robinson, *Mega-Small Church*. Their website is http://crosspointri.wpengine.com.

89. The organization "is an association of social service agencies, community organizations, educational institutions and businesses striving to strengthen the City of Newport by prioritizing and supporting the needs of children, families and individuals." Specifically, the coalition is working to ameliorate local issues like "substance abuse and school absenteeism." See https://newportpartnership.org/.

not) by letting them educate the congregation on their mission and we spent a month with each group praying with them, serving them, and giving financial grants toward their mission. For instance, EFC served Looking Upwards, "a private, nonprofit agency offering a wide array of services to adults with developmental disabilities and children with special healthcare needs."[90] We volunteered at their annual golf-tournament fundraiser, built a stone patio for some precious ladies in one of their residential homes, prayed with the program participants, and gave a financial gift. Three of the beneficiaries now attend our church. (Don't tell anyone, but they're my favorite parishoners!)

- **"Common Ground" in Missouri:** A group that draws together "pro-choice and pro-life leaders to discuss shared interests such as preventing unwanted pregnancies."[91] Surprisingly, they "worked together to support state legislation to pay for pregnant drug addicts. The abortion clinic opened on premises adoption services to provide an alternative to unwanted pregnancies."[92]

- **CityServe (Portland, Oregon):** Five hundred evangelical congregations, led by evangelist Kevin Palau, collaborated with Sam Adams, Portland, Oregon's openly gay mayor, and other groups, to assist "the city do everything from renovating parks, to counseling victims of sex trafficking and feeding the homeless."[93] This led to a burgeoning partnership centered on addressing five major needs in their city: hunger, homelessness, public schools, the healthcare system, and environmental care.[94]

This is a tiny sampling of all the examples that exist. But hopefully I have provided some concrete ideas to get started with. Nevertheless, there remain numerous ways reconciling communities and coalitions may grow and develop: a work may start as a coalition (e.g., a nonprofit collaborating with a local congregation), or the Spirit may lead a church to start another church (e.g., NewSong starting verges in Bangkok) or social agency (e.g., Voice of Calvary opening legal services) which pinpoints meeting specific needs.

90. See https://www.lookingupwards.org.

91. Former US Senator Jack Danforth, cited in Inazu, *Confident Pluralism*, 119–20.

92. Danforth, cited in Inazu, *Confident Pluralism*, 119–20.

93. Inazu, *Confident Pluralism*, 120–21.

94. See Palau, *Unlikely*.

CONCLUSION

The superstructure of reconciling practices encompasses three essential habits: reconciling prayer, reconciling rhetoric, and forming reconciling communities and coalitions. Prayer is the fiber-optic network linking Christians to the Trinity and one another, and it is the spiritual weapon that enables reconcilers to both lament alienation and injustice and intercede before the King. Second, reconciling rhetoric acknowledges the potency of words to create or destroy and so fosters a posture of repentance before the world. Finally, reconciling communities and coalitions pursue collaborative and fresh opportunities that bring an embodied gospel witness to each place.

Questions for Reflection

1. Of the three reconciling practices, which do you feel most comfortable with or drawn to, and why? Which habit do you feel least comfortable with and why?

2. In your prayer life (or that of your congregation), do you perceive elements of lament, intercession, and transformation?

3. Can you recall an incident when you observed a negative post on social media? How did it make you feel?

4. Does your congregation or organization engage in reconciling partnerships or coalitions? Have you ever dreamed of starting a new initiative? If so, what is holding you back?

Practical Next Steps

1. Spend one week praying through Lamentations or a psalm of lament. Read it out loud, slowly, carefully, and meditatively. Write in a journal any phrases or emotions that catch your attention.

2. Research and visit at least three social service agencies within a ten-mile radius of your home. Who do they care for (their clientele) and what needs do they meet? What might it look like if your group of friends, Bible study/community group, or church engaged this organization through prayer, financial resources, or volunteer hours?

Conclusion: A Redux, Recasting, and Reconciling Commission

Redux: August 20, 2017

WE NOW CONCLUDE WHERE we started: with a prayer rally promoting reconciliation and peace.

It was August 20, 2017, a little over thirteen months after the fateful events of July 2016. Once again a multicolored, multigenerational, and multidenominational collection of around 120 Christians and people of good will[1] gathered in front of Newport City Hall to "Unite To Pray Against Hatred." Unlike the previous rally, this one was planned days in advance, and was an intentional response to the national uproar ignited by the "Unite the Right" rally in Charlottesville, Virginia, on Saturday, August 12, 2017. In an alarming development, "violence erupted . . . after hundreds of white nationalists and their supporters who gathered for a rally over plans to remove a Confederate statue were met by counter-protestors, leading Virginia's governor to declare a state of emergency."[2] Tragically, three people lost their lives that day: counter protestor Heather D. Heyer died when she was hit by a car in an act of violence, and Virginia state troopers Lt. H. Jay Cullen and Trooper Berke M. M. Bates died when their helicopter, which was monitoring the protests, crashed.

That week our nation was bombarded by a wide array of volatile emotions: fear, outrage, tension, a sense of looming chaos. It was time again to convene people together around the Great Reconciler, Jesus Christ, and the profoundly uniting act of prayer. Rather than recount what unfolded, which is done elsewhere,[3] I want to share the event schedule and remarks, which convey the vision many of us sought to cast (which I've edited for clarity):

1. A strategic unit used to catalyze change—see Acts 1:15.
2. Katz, "Unrest in Virginia."
3. Please feel free to read these articles: Hill, "In Newport," and Gomes, "Rising up

131

1—Purpose of Gathering/Opening Statement: Paul Hoffman

This is a peaceful gathering of people of faith, organized by local churches in Newport County. We are here in obedience to Jesus's words:

- "Love your enemies and pray for those who persecute you" (Matt 5:44).

- We are also inspired by the words of Martin Luther King Jr.: "Darkness cannot drive out darkness; only light can do that. Hate cannot drive out hate; only love can do that."[4]

- This is *not* a partisan, political gathering or protest. Please refrain from critiquing our politicians.

- This is a prayer meeting. We are asking God to heal our nation, and to mend our divides and to cleanse hate and pour God's love, forgiveness, and reconciliation into our hearts.

- However, we state unequivocally, that racism, anti-Semitism, misogyny, bigotry, and hate, in all shapes and forms, including white supremacy, neo-Nazism, and the KKK are wrong, shameful, sinful, unbiblical, and unchristian.

- In a moment, Pastor Lauri Johnson of Community Baptist Church will open the meeting in prayer. Then we will have one minute of silence to mourn the passing of three people last Saturday in Charlottesville: Heather Heyer, and Virginia state patrol troopers Jay Cullen and Burke Bates.

- Afterwards, we will pray through these points, led first by pastors, then open to a few prayers from the crowd. The churches represented are Evangelical Friends Church of Newport, Community Baptist Church, Crosspoint Church, Oceanpointe Church, Portsmouth United Methodist Church, His Providence Church, and Calvary United Methodist Church.

2—Lauri Johnson leads moment of silence.

3—Pastor-led prayer:

A—Read Matt 5:3–4: Jesus said "Blessed are the poor in Spirit and those who mourn." As Christians, we repent of our failures. We have been angry and divisive. We have forgotten the poor, weak, and downtrodden. We have not

---

against hate."

4. King, *Strength to Love*, 37.

always stood up for justice. We have been distracted and complacent.

B—Read Matt 5:21–24; 7:1–5: Jesus said "do not be angry or judge others." We pray God will remove ungodly anger from our hearts and judgmental or self-righteous attitudes.

C—Read Matt 5:9: "blessed are the peacemakers." We pray we live into our calling as peacemakers.

D—Read Matt 5:13–16: "you are the salt of the earth, you are the light of the world, you are a city on a hill."

E—Read Matt 5:43–48: "Love your enemies and pray for those who persecute you." We pray to love our enemies and pray for those who persecute us.

F—We pray for those individuals and groups with hate in their hearts.

4—Sing "This Little Light of Mine" out loud.

5—Paul Hoffman closes in prayer.

As I reflect on this event, I can detect aspects of the three parts of the reconciling bridge:

1. It was place-based. Although the incident that sparked national outrage occurred hundreds of miles away in Charlottesville, God's image-bearers inhabiting Newport, Rhode Island, were upset, and desired a healthy way to process and express their complex emotions.

2. The rally evoked the relational nature of the Trinity (the foundation): a diverse group of Christians and churches sought to connect horizontally and vertically: They pursued *koinonia* with one another by praying together to the triune Godhead for peace to prevail in the face of turmoil and violence.

3. Our gathering embodied the teaching of 2 Cor 5 and a theology of reconciliation (the substructure). We announced we congregated not to pour gasoline on an existing conflagration, but rather in a modest attempt "to heal our nation, and to mend our divides." Further, we prayed through sections of Matt 5 as a witness to the community and wider world that we need and look to Jesus to help us live into our identity as his "peacemakers."

4. Our audience engaged in reconciling practices (the superstructure) by praying in public. We lamented the sins of racism, bigotry, etc., interceded for our nation and community, and through singing, cast an alternative narrative: "This Little Light of Mine, I'm gonna let it shine!" We also used reconciling rhetoric: no hateful speech was allowed, only constructive and scriptural speech, and this was modeled by the clergy who led. Lastly, for a few hours we formed a Beloved Community, a coalition of gospel hope. We accomplished this because partnerships and relationships had previously been established, and so our train drove over the existing tracks.

Now, I acknowledge skeptics may read about this event, and think, "OK, fine. But that's just one event that succeeded in bringing comity in a time of strife. What difference will it make in the long run?" That objection reminds me of the old tale about the starfishes stranded on the beach. You can throw one back in the ocean and indeed you've only changed the destiny of one creature, while thousands more remain marooned. And so I agree it's fair to ask: did the "Unite to Pray Against Hatred" rally make a long-term impact in our region or wider society? Did it help foster shalom in the face of systemic injustice? The easy and clear answer is, "no." We might have saved just one starfish.

However, when I step back to scan and consider the annals of history, I feel confident stating this: one action contains within it the kernel of possibility, that is, now or later, it might initiate a chain reaction that ripples through the larger system. Or in the very least, one reconciling action can gesture that change—something better—is imaginable. There are Rev 7 moments that puncture our gloomiest despair, and signpost to heaven. An alternate reality pulses somewhere—this is a sliver of hope we can latch onto.

Reconciling starts here. Yet it is animated by a sublime vision rooted in a captivating story.

Recasting MLK Jr.'s "Beloved Community"

In my eleventh grade honors history class (shout out to Mrs. Northway!), we were tasked with delivering a monologue impersonating a historical figure in modern American history. I chose Martin Luther King Jr.'s iconic, "I Have a Dream" speech. (I am *so* glad iPhones didn't exist in 1995 to record this!) I hate to make this confession, but as a white high school student from Maine, with no public speaking, acting, or homiletical training, I attempted to parrot King's speech completely: his accent, cadence, pace, punch, etc.[5]

Setting my embarrassment aside, even then, King's eloquent words stirred my soul in a way I could not understand or articulate. To this day—with my comprehension perhaps slightly more developed—a mini-geyser of emotion erupts inside me as I recall this masterpiece of rhetoric and prophetic call to action. Why? I share Dr. King's conviction that we must strive for a more just world *now*, so my children, and all children, and the generations to follow, "will one day live in a nation where they will not be judged by the color of their skin but by the content of their character."[6] And yes, I long to be completely immersed in King's vision for the "Beloved Community": that people of different ethnicities, sexes, classes, nationalities, educational experiences, abilities (typical and atypical) not just tolerate one other, but value and love one another as image-bearers of the triune God. I ache for everyone to prayerfully enjoin one another in *koinonia*, and in doing so become images and representations of the Trinity's interpenetrating mutuality, all while maintaining their diversity.

I wish this for me.

I wish this for the congregation I shepherd.

Yet my urgency has increased for two reasons: my past and my future.

First, I recently discovered I am the descendent of two world-renowned enemies. Through my mother's lineage, I am the ancestor of King Edward I of England, known as "Edward Longshanks" and the "Hammer of the Scots." Through my father's lineage, I just so happen to be the ancestor of William Wallace, known as "Braveheart," the Scottish knight who fought against England in the First War of Scottish Independence. Around 1305, Wallace was captured and King Edward I had him hanged, drawn, and quartered for high treason against the crown. As I write this, I am wearing a necklace that contains a metal crest representing Wallace[7] next to a penny minted by the government of King Edward III.[8] My necklace reminds me that although my forbears were adversaries, the animosity ends with me. Yea the Great Reconciler, Jesus Christ, has made me a new person, holds my heart in his hands,

---

5. Let the record stand: I did not attempt naked cultural appropriation or "blackface," which we now know is racially offensive.

6. King Jr., "I Have a Dream."

7. The Crawford family crest. Wallace's mother, Margaret Crawford, is my ancestor.

8. Edward III is a relative of Edward I. The coin was minted in England, circa the mid-1300s.

and his grace redeems my lineage and grants me the message, ministry, and identity of reconciliation.

Second, I am the father of two strapping and sensitive sons. How can I claim to be faithful—as a passionate Christ-follower, dedicated reconciler, devoted father, and committed pastor—if I am unable to pass on the DNA of a reconciler to my current progeny and their unimagined future generations? This question haunts me.

Nevertheless, I am grateful to God for the ability to discern hints taking hold: my sons have initiated and developed relationships with classmates from Saudi Arabia, Tunisia, Mexico, and Poland, along with some who might be considered "unpopular" by societies' standards due to a broken home, disabilities, or atypical tendencies. Of this I am proud. Yet just like their father, they are fallible creatures, and I have heard them utter words and phrases that caused me dismay, and even shame.

My ongoing desire for them is that they will consistently recognize and engage the biblical narrative unfolding before us of Creator, creation, alienation, reconciliation, and final creation. Once they know the Creator, the Reconciler, the Healer, the Lamb who was slain who sits on the throne, they will join his trajectory, his flow toward the consummation of all things. Then, by God's grace and in his timing, they can devote their lives to promoting reconciliation and building bridges across difference. Then, by God's mercy and power, they too will join me in embracing the message, ministry, and identity of reconciliation. Although I am delighted to be an ordained minister of the gospel, I am convinced this can be accomplished whatever their vocation or profession—reconciling is an all-encompassing worldview, attitude, and lifestyle. To be sure, at present, the nations are begging for courageous champions who will spread shalom amidst the places they inhabit. Who will answer the call? Who will forsake the vainglory of individual success to sacrifice one's life for a "surpassingly great revelation?"[9] If we deny this call, we may breathe, but we'll never countenance the fullness of life the triune Godhead promises.

I now bid adieu in the best way I know how: with words of blessing and instruction. They are not intended exclusively for my sons, Landon and Kelan, but for every child and every generation that will hear the call, and receive the reconciling mantle.

9. 2 Cor 12:7.

A reconciling commission to my children

To my Beloved Sons:

You have been invited into the most perplexing and pure journey that exists: to be a peacemaker, reconciler, and bridge builder amidst a world inundated by fear, hate, and the rampant schisms fueled by the "-isms."

Although this is a sojourn all Christians are called to undertake, not all possess the pluck, wherewithal, or hutzpah to commence upon or continually commit to this slender trail.

Be not paralyzed nor deterred. Take one step. Another. A third. Establish a rhythm, a pattern. Remember: you are simply following the previous path of Jesus.

Beware: you will come across potholes and cavernous traps. You are less likely to be slowed than swallowed whole. The snares are legion: love of self, greed, lust, self-gratification, resume-and-career-building; Narcissus's latest reflecting pools (e.g., social media apps, video games), etc.

When you're tempted to exclude, choose to embrace.

When you're tempted to judge based on a person's outer crust, plunge beneath into his or her lithosphere, mantle, and core.

When you're tempted to distraction, reset your coordinates and your jaw . . . determination is in short supply in our addled-by-hyperactivity society.

Never forget: you labor not in vain. The Reconciler has risen! He has gone ahead to prepare the new creation for you.

Until the eschaton emerges—that eternal light first cresting, then cascading over our frail horizon—chronos time . . . ticks . . . ticks . . . ticks.

Your vase still shimmers with the precious drops of the healing balm of Gilead.

Go, and pour it, and yourself, out.

In name of *Abba* (Daddy), *Yeshua* (Jesus), and *Paracletos* (Advocate), Amen.

Bibliography

Abramowitz, Alan I., and Steven W. Webster. "All Politics is National: The Rise of Negative Partisanship and the Nationalization of U.S. House and Senate Elections in the 21st Century." Paper presented at Annual Meeting of the Midwest Political Science Association, Chicago, Illinois, April 16–19, 2015. http://stevenwwebster.com/research/all_politics_is_national.pdf.

Alexander, Michelle. *The New Jim Crow: Mass Incarceration in the Age of Colorblindness.* New York: New Press, 2012.

Allianz. "Top 20 megacities by population." Last modified March 16, 2015. Accessed January 9, 2020. https://www.allianz.com/en/about_us/open-knowledge/topics/demography/articles/150316-top-20-megacities-by-population.html/.

Arndt, William F., et al., eds. *A Greek-English Lexicon of the New Testament and Other Early Christian Literature.* 2nd ed. Chicago: University of Chicago Press, 1979.

Assayas, Michka. *Bono: In Conversation with Michka Assayas.* New York: Riverhead, 2005.

A. T. Kearney. *2012 Global Cities Index and Emerging Cities Outlook.* Chicago: Kearney, 2013. http://www.atkearney.com/documents/10192/dfedfc4c-8a62-4162-90e5-2a3f14f0da3a.

Barker, Kenneth L., ed. *Zondervan NIV Study Bible.* Grand Rapids: Zondervan, 2002.

Barry, John D., and Lazarus Wentz, eds. *The Lexham Bible Dictionary.* Bellingham, WA: Lexham, 2012.

Bartholomew, Craig G., and Michael W. Goheen. *The Drama of Scripture: Finding Our Place in the Biblical Story.* Grand Rapids: Baker Academic, 2004.

Bauckham, Richard. *Bible and Mission: Christian Witness in a Postmodern World.* Milton Keynes, UK: Paternoster, 2005.

Beitler III, James E. *Seasoned Speech: Rhetoric in the Life of the Church.* Downers Grove, IL: InterVarsity, 2019.

Belmore, Ryan. "Video: NAACP Prayer Vigil for Racial Justice Held in Newport." *Whatsupnewp,* June 1, 2020. https://whatsupnewp.com/2020/06/video-naacp-prayer-vigil-for-racial-justice-held-in-newport/.

Bennett, Arthur G. *The Valley of Vision: A Collection of Puritan Prayers and Devotions.* Edinburgh: Banner of Truth, 1975.

Berkhof, Hendrikus. *The Doctrine of the Holy Spirit.* The Annie Kinkead Warfield Lectures, 1963–1964. Atlanta: John Knox, 1964.

Bevans, Stephen B. *Models of Contextual Theology.* Faith and Cultures. Rev. ed. Maryknoll, NY: Orbis, 2011.

Bevans, Stephen B., and Roger Schroeder. *Constants in Context: A Theology of Mission for Today.* American Society of Missiology Series 30. Maryknoll, NY: Orbis, 2004.

Black, Amy E., ed. *Five Views on the Church and Politics.* Grand Rapids: Zondervan, 2015.

Bloesch, Donald G. *God, Authority, and Salvation*. Vol. 1, *Essentials of Evangelical Theology*. New York: HarperCollins, 1978.

Bosch, David J. *Transforming Mission: Paradigm Shifts in the Theology of Mission*. American Society of Missiology Series 16. Maryknoll, NY: Orbis, 1991.

Branch, Jim. *The Blue Book: A Devotional Guide for Every Season of your Life*. North Charleston, SC: CreateSpace, 2016.

Bretherton, Luke. *Christianity and Contemporary Politics: The Conditions and Possibilities of Faithful Witness*. Chichester, UK: Wiley-Blackwell, 2009.

Bryant, David. "Affirming Christ's Ascension on the National Day of Prayer." Proclaim Hope. https://www.proclaimhope.org/media/pdf/IFA%20Apr05pg3.pdf.

———. *Christ Is NOW!: 7 Groundbreaking Keys to Help You Explore and Experience the Spectacular Supremacy of God's Son Today*. New Providence, NJ: New Providence, 2017.

Cameron, Helen. *Resourcing Mission: Practical Theology for Changing Churches*. London: SCM, 2010.

Cameron, Julia E. M., ed. *Christ Our Reconciler: Gospel, Church, World: The Third Lausanne Congress on World Evangelization*. Downers Grove, IL: InterVarsity, 2012.

Cape Town Diamond Museum. "Does a Diamond With More Facets Sparkle More?" https://www.capetowndiamondmuseum.org/blog/2017/05/does-a-diamond-with-more-facets-sparkle-more/.

Cartwright, Mark. "Kali." Ancient History Encyclopedia. https://www.ancient.eu/Kali/.

Clark, Donald. "10X Loupe for Gemologists and Jewelers." International Gem Society. Accessed January 9, 2020. https://www.gemsociety.org/article/10x-loupe-the-gemologists-best-friend/.

Cloud, Henry, and John Townsend. *Boundaries: When to Say Yes and When to Say No to Take Control of Your Life*. Grand Rapids: Zondervan, 1992.

Coates, Ta-Nehisi. *We Were Eight Years in Power: An American Tragedy*. New York: One World, 2018.

Cohen, Darryl. "Population Trends in Incorporated Places: 2000 to 2013." United States Census Bureau. https://www.census.gov/library/publications/2015/demo/p25-1142.html.

"College Graduates live longer, CDC report shows." *ABC 7*, May 16, 2012. http://abc7.com/archive/8664380/.

Comer, John Mark. "The Case for a Digital Asceticism." Sermon, Bridgetown Church, Portland, OR, November 13, 2019. https://practicingtheway.org/teaching/the-case-for-a-digital-asceticism.

Cook, Lindsey. "Seriously, Go to College." *U.S. News & World Report*, August 17, 2015. https://www.usnews.com/news/blogs/data-mine/2015/08/17/study-benefits-of-a-college-degree-are-historically-high.

Congar, Yves M. J. *I Believe in the Holy Spirit: Lord and Giver of Life*. Vol. 2. Translated by David Smith. New York: Seabury, 1983.

Crouch, Andy. *The Tech-Wise Family: Everyday Steps for Putting Technology in its Place*. Grand Rapids: Baker, 2017.

Damon, Laura. "Peaceful vigil held in Newport in wake of George Floyd's killing." *The Newport Daily News*, June 1, 2020. https://www.newportri.com/news/20200601/peaceful-vigil-held-in-newport-in-wake-of-george-floydrsquos-killing.

Davenport, Keith M., ed. *Conversations on Holiness*. Kansas City: Beacon Hill, 2013.

Davis, Kay. "Class and Leisure at America's First Resort." Xroads. http://xroads.virginia.edu/
~mao1/davis/newport/timeline/events_timeline.html.

DeFranza, Megan K. *Sex Difference in Christian Theology: Male, Female, and Intersex in the Image of God.* Grand Rapids: Eerdmans, 2015.

de Gruchy, John W. *Reconciliation: Restoring Justice.* Minneapolis: Fortress, 2002.

Ellul, Jacques. *The Meaning of the City.* Grand Rapids: Eerdmans, 1970.

Elsworth, Peter C. T. "Newport's Festival of Hope honors 9/11 first responders with music, food and kid's activities." *Providence Journal,* September 7, 2016. https://www.providencejournal.com/entertainmentlife/20160907/newports-festival-of-hope-honors-911-first-responders-with-music-food-and-kids-activities.

Etehad, Melissa. "'I Don't Want You to Get Shooted': Philando Castile Video Shows Reaction of Girlfriend's 4-Year-Old Daughter." *Los Angeles Times,* June 22, 2017. http://www.latimes.com/nation/la-na-video-diamond-reynolds-daughter-20170622-story.html.

Emerson, Michael O., and Christian Smith. *Divided by Faith: Evangelical Religion and the Problem of Race in America.* Oxford: Oxford University Press, 2000.

The Evangelical Friends Church-Eastern Region. "Faith and Practice." https://www.efcer.org/media/1/9/Faith%20and%20Practice%202018%20Edition%20(Approved%20 7_24_18).pdf.

Fee, Gordon D., and Douglas Stuart. *How to Read the Bible for All Its Worth.* 2nd ed. Grand Rapids: Zondervan, 1993.

Fitch, David E. *Faithful Presence: Seven Disciplines that Shape the Church for Mission.* Downers Grove, IL: InterVarsity, 2016.

Foust, Thomas F., et al., eds. *A Scandalous Prophet: The Way of Mission After Newbigin.* Grand Rapids: Eerdmans, 2001.

Flynn, Sean. "Hundreds gather at Festival of Hope to remember, honor victims of 9/11." *Newport (RI) Daily News,* September 12, 2016. https://www.newportri.com/f4abf3bb-8a42-5622-885d-123ee9b81124.html.

———. "Kids Count Eyes Poverty in Newport." *Newport (RI) Daily News,* October 6, 2015. http://www.newportri.com/newportdailynews/news/page_one/kids-count-eyes-poverty-in-newport/article_7fdc7fef-d95a-564c-a2f2-e42c25614f17.html.

Fuder, John, ed. *A Heart for the City: Effective Ministries to the Urban Community.* Chicago: Moody, 1999.

Fung, Ronald Y. K. *The Epistle to the Galatians.* New International Commentary on the New Testament. Grand Rapids: Eerdmans, 1988.

Galvin, Gaby. "Coronavirus Survey: One-Third of U.S. Adults Have Symptoms of Depression or Anxiety." *US News & World Report,* May 27, 2020. https://www.usnews.com/news/healthiest-communities/articles/2020-05-27/one-third-of-us-adults-have-signs-of-depression-anxiety-during-pandemic.

George, Timothy. *Galatians: An Exegetical and Theological Exposition Of Holy Scripture.* New American Commentary 30. Nashville: Holman, 1994.

Gibbons, Dave. *The Monkey and the Fish: Liquid Leadership for a Third-Culture Church.* Leadership Network Innovation Series 5. Grand Rapids: Zondervan, 2009.

Glaeser, Edward. *Triumph of the City: How our Greatest Invention Makes us Richer, Smarter, Greener, Healthier, and Happier.* New York: Penguin, 2012.

Goheen, Michael W. *Introducing Christian Mission Today: Scripture, History and Issues.* Downers Grove, IL: InterVarsity, 2014.

Gomes, Derek. "Rising up against hate." *Newport Daily News*, August 21, 2017. https://www.newportri.com/bf9b0df5-f541-536f-a548-15c3b0af381c.html.

Gorringe, T. J. *A Theology of the Built Environment: Justice, Empowerment, Redemption.* Cambridge: Cambridge University Press, 2002.

Gornik, Mark R. *To Live in Peace: Biblical Faith and the Changing Inner City.* Grand Rapids: Eerdmans, 2002.

The Government of the Bahamas. Ministry of Foreign Affairs. "Ministry of Foreign Affairs and Immigration Issues Travel Advisory for Bahamians Traveling to United States of America." July 8, 2016. http://mofa.gov.bs/ministry-of-foreign-affairs-and-immigration-issues-travel-advisory-for-bahamians-traveling-to-united-states-of-america/.

Green, Joel B., et al., eds. *Dictionary of Jesus and the Gospels: A Compendium of Contemporary Biblical Scholarship.* 2nd ed. IVP Bible Dictionary Series. Downers Grove, IL: InterVarsity, 2013.

Gunton, Colin E. *The Promise of Trinitarian Theology.* 2nd ed. London: T. & T. Clark, 1997.

Hastings, Ross. *Missional God, Missional Church: Hope for Re-evangelizing the West.* Downers Grove, IL: InterVarsity, 2012.

Hawthorne, Gerald F., et al., eds. *Dictionary of Paul and His Letters: A Compendium of Contemporary Biblical Scholarship.* IVP Bible Dictionary Series. Downers Grove, IL: InterVarsity, 2015.

Heimans, Jeremy, and Henry Timms. *New Power: How Anyone Can Persuade, Mobilize and Succeed in Our Chaotic, Connected Age.* New York: Doubleday, 2018.

Henderson, Daniel. *Old Paths, New Power: Awakening Your Church through Prayer and the Ministry of the Word.* Chicago: Moody, 2016.

Hess, Tom. *The Restoration of the Tabernacle of David: Preparing the Way for the King of Glory.* Jerusalem: Progressive Vision, 2005.

Hill, John. "In Newport, Faithful from Area Churches Gather to Stand up to Hatred." *Providence Journal*, August 21, 2017. https://www.providencejournal.com/news/20170820/in-newport-faithful-from-area-churches-gather-to-stand-up-to-hatred.

History of Bridges. "Structure, Components and Parts of Bridge." Accessed January 9, 2020. http://www.historyofbridges.com/facts-about-bridges/bridge-parts/.

Hoffman, Paul. "A Critical Assessment of the Practical Theology of 'Urban Missional Engagement' with Particular Reference to Redeemer Presbyterian Church." PhD thesis, University of Manchester, 2017.

———. "Activism 101: How Churches Can Respond to the Death of George Floyd." *ChurchLeaders*, June 15, 2020. https://churchleaders.com/outreach-missions/outreach-missions-articles/377212-activism-101-how-churches-can-respond-to-the-death-of-george-floyd.html.

———. "A Way Forward." *Newport This Week*, June 4, 2020. https://www.newportthisweek.com/articles/a-way-forward/?fbclid=IwAR2PI8xGj937dewvRE3OrQdiecXF5DnpUm6D6bTa6fNB3RdP1v8fVl_6FKk.

———. "Polar Views of the City: Jacques Ellul vs. Timothy Keller." *Occasional Bulletin of the Evangelical Missiological Society* 30, no. 2 (2017) 12–15.

Hoffman, Paul A. "The Missiological Debate over Acts 2:14–21: Examining Differing Hermeneutics and Implications." Paper presented at the 70th Annual Meeting of the Evangelical Theological Society, Denver, CO, November 13, 2018.

Hoffman, Paul A. and Matthew D. Kim. "Four Ways Church Leaders Can Inspire Racial Healing." *Influence Magazine*, June 10, 2020. https://influencemagazine.com/en/Practice/Four-Ways-Church-Leaders-Can-Inspire-Racial-Healing.

Holley, Peter. "A Black Man Went Undercover Online as a White Supremacist. This Is What He Learned." *Washington Post*, April 8, 2019. https://www.washingtonpost.com/news/the-switch/wp/2017/08/24/a-black-man-went-undercover-as-a-digital-white-supremacist-this-is-what-he-learned/?noredirect=on&utm_term=.95eaef7451a2.

Hunter, James Davison. *To Change the World: The Irony, Tragedy, and Possibility of Christianity in the Late Modern World*. New York: Oxford University Press, 2010.

Inazu, John D. *Confident Pluralism: Surviving and Thriving through Deep Difference*. Chicago: University of Chicago Press, 2016.

Inge, John. *A Christian Theology of Place*. Explorations in Practical, Pastoral and Empirical Theology. London: Routledge, 2003.

Jenkins, Jack. "'Nones' now as big as evangelicals, Catholics in the US." *National Catholic Reporter*, March 22, 2019. https://www.ncronline.org/news/people/nones-now-big-evangelicals-catholics-us.

Jennings, Willie James. *The Christian Imagination: Theology and the Origins of Race*. New Haven, CT: Yale University Press, 2011.

Katangole, Emmanuel, and Chris Rice. *Reconciling All Things: a Christian Vision for Justice, Peace and Healing*. Resources for Reconciliation. Downers Grove, IL: InterVarsity, 2008.

Katz, Andrew, ed. "Unrest in Virginia: Clashes Over a Show of White Nationalism Charlottesville Turn Deadly." *Time*. Accessed January 9, 2020. https://time.com/charlottesville-white-nationalist-rally-clashes/.

Keller, Timothy. *Center Church: Doing Balanced, Gospel-Centered Ministry in Your City*. Grand Rapids: Zondervan, 2012.

———. *Counterfeit Gods: The Empty Promises of Money, Sex, and Power, and the Only Hope That Matters*. New York: Penguin, 2011.

———. *Encounters with Jesus: Unexpected Answers to Life's Biggest Questions*. New York: Penguin, 2015.

———. *Galatians For You*. God's Word For You. Epsom, UK: The Good Book Company, 2017.

———. *Generous Justice: How God's Grace Makes Us Just*. New York: Penguin, 2010.

———. *Hidden Christmas: The Surprising Truth Behind the Birth of Christ*. New York: Penguin, 2018.

———. *Prodigal God: Recovering the Heart of the Christian Faith*. New York: Penguin, 2011.

———. *Walking with God through Pain and Suffering*. New York: Penguin, 2015.

———. *Why God Made Cities*. New York: City to City, 2013. https://gospelinlife.com/downloads/why-god-made-cities/.

Kevan, Ernest F. *What the Scriptures Teach*. Darlington, UK: Evangelical, 1966.

Khanna, Parag. "Beyond City Limits." *Foreign Policy*, August 6, 2010. http://www.foreignpolicy.com/articles/2010/08/16/beyond_city_limits.

Kim, Kirsteen. *The Holy Spirit in the World: A Global Conversation*. Maryknoll, NY: Orbis, 2007.

Kim, Matthew D. and Gibson, Scott M., eds. *The Big Idea Companion for Preaching and Teaching: A Guide from Genesis to Revelation*. Grand Rapids: Baker Academic, forthcoming.

King, Martin Luther, Jr. "I Have a Dream." Speech at the March on Washington, Washington, DC, August 28, 1963. https://www.archives.gov/files/press/exhibits/dream-speech.pdf.

———. *Strength to Love*. New York: Harper & Row, 1963.

Kline, Meredith G. *Kingdom Prologue: Genesis Foundations for a Covenantal Worldview*. Eugene, OR: Wipf & Stock, 2006.

Kotkin, Joel. *The City: A Global History*. New York: Modern Library, 2005.

Kottasova, Ivana. "These 8 Men Are Richer than 3.6 Billion People Combined." *CNN Business*, January 17, 2017. http://money.cnn.com/2017/01/15/news/economy/oxfam-income-inequality-men/.

Koyzis, David. *Political Visions & Illusions: A Survey & Christian Critique of Contemporary Ideologies*. 2nd ed. Grand Rapids: InterVarsity, 2019.

Kwon, Duke, and Gabe Lyons. "Race Reparations with Duke Kwon." Q Ideas, June 14, 2018. https://vimeo.com/275016018.

Langone, Alix. "#MeToo and Time's Up Founders Explain the Difference Between the 2 Movements—And How They're Alike." *Time*, March 22, 2018. https://time.com/5189945/whats-the-difference-between-the-metoo-and-times-up-movements/.

Lederach, John Paul. *Reconcile: Conflict Transformation for Ordinary Christians*. Harrisonburg, VA: Herald, 2014.

Lee-Barnewall, Michelle. *Neither Complementarian nor Egalitarian: A Kingdom Corrective to the Evangelical Gender Debate*. Grand Rapids: Baker Academic, 2016.

Leong, David P. *Race and Place: How Urban Geography Shapes the Journey to Reconciliation*. Downers Grove, IL: InterVarsity, 2017.

Lewis, C. S. *The Weight of Glory*. New York: HarperOne, 2001.

Linthicum, Robert C. *City of God, City of Satan: A Biblical Theology of the Urban Church*. Grand Rapids: Zondervan, 1991.

Ma, Julie C., and Wonsuk Ma. *Mission in the Spirit: Towards a Pentecostal/Charismatic Missiology*. Regnum Studies in Mission. Eugene, OR: Wipf & Stock, 2011.

Mahdawi, Arwa. "'Class-passing': how do you learn the rules of being rich?" *Guardian*, February 1, 2018. https://www.theguardian.com/us-news/2018/feb/01/poor-americans-poverty-rich-class.

Marsh, Charles. *The Beloved Community: How Faith Shapes Social Justice, from the Civil Rights Movement to Today*. New York: Basic, 2006.

Mason, Lilliana. "Ideologues without Issues: The Polarizing Consequences of Ideological Identities." *Public Opinion Quarterly* 82, no. s1 (2018) 866–887.

———. *Uncivil Agreement: How Politics Became Our Identity*. Chicago: University of Chicago Press, 2018.

McBride, Jennifer M. *The Church for the World: A Theology of Public Witness*. New York: Oxford University Press, 2014.

McIntosh, Gary L., and Alan McMahan. *Being the Church in a Multi-Ethnic Community: Why It Matters and How It Works*. Indianapolis: Wesleyan, 2012.

Moltmann Jürgen. *The Trinity and the Kingdom: The Doctrine of God*. Minneapolis: Fortress, 1993.

Morris, Leon. *The Apostolic Preaching of the Cross*. Grand Rapids: Eerdmans, 1965.

———. *The Gospel According to John*. Rev. ed. New International Commentary on the New Testament. Grand Rapids: Eerdmans, 1995.

Mundy, Liza. "Why Is Silicon Valley So Awful to Women?" *Atlantic*, April 2019. https://www.theatlantic.com/magazine/archive/2017/04/why-is-silicon-valley-so-awful-to-women/517788/.

Murray, Stuart. *Post-Christendom*. Waynesboro, GA: Authentic Media, 2004.

Muscato, Christopher. "Newport Bridge: History & Construction." Study.com. Accessed January 9, 2020. https://study.com/academy/lesson/newport-bridge-history-construction.html.

Nash, June, ed. *Social Movements: An Anthropological Reader*. Blackwell Readers in Anthropology. Malden, MA: Blackwell, 2008.

National Sexual Violence Resource Center. "Statistics." https://www.nsvrc.org/statistics.

Newbigin, Lesslie. *Foolishness to the Greeks: The Gospel and Western Culture*. Grand Rapids: Eerdmans, 1987.

———. *The Gospel in a Pluralist Society*. Grand Rapids: Eerdmans, 1989.

———. *The Open Secret: An Introduction to the Theology of Mission*. Grand Rapids: Eerdmans, 1995.

———. *Trinitarian Doctrine for Today's Mission*. 1988. Reprint, Eugene, OR: Wipf & Stock, 2006.

Newport, Cal. *Digital Minimalism: Choosing a Focused Life in a Noisy World*. New York: Penguin, 2019.

Open Doors USA. "Christian Persecution." Accessed January 9, 2020. http://www.opendoorsusa.org/christian-persecution/.

Otis Jr., George. *Informed Intercession: Transforming Your Community Through Spiritual Mapping and Strategic Prayer*. Ventura, CA: Regal, 1999.

Ott, Craig, and Stephen J. Strauss. *Encountering Theology of Mission: Biblical Foundations, Historical Developments, and Contemporary Issues*. Encountering Mission. Grand Rapids: Baker Academic, 2010.

Packer, J. I. *Evangelism and the Sovereignty of God*. Downers Grove, IL: InterVarsity, 2012.

———. *Knowing God*. Downers Grove, IL: InterVarsity, 1993.

Palau, Kevin. *Unlikely: Setting Aside Our Differences to Live out the Gospel*. New York: Howard, 2016.

Payne, Ruby K. *A Framework for Understanding Poverty*. 4th ed. Highlands, TX: aha! Process, 2005.

Perkins, John. *With Justice for All: A Strategy for Community Development*. Ventura, CA: Regal, 1982.

Pew Research Center. "Religious Hostilities Reach Six-Year High." Pew Research Center's Religion & Public Life Project. January 14, 2014. https://www.pewforum.org/2014/01/14/religious-hostilities-reach-six-year-high/.

Pier, Mac. *Spiritual Leadership in the Global City*. Birmingham, AL: New Hope, 2008.

Pier, Mac, and Katie Sweeting. *The Power of a City at Prayer: What Happens When Churches Unite for Renewal*. Downers Grove, IL: InterVarsity, 2002.

Preservation Society of Newport County. "Our Mission." http://www.newportmansions.org/about-us/our-mission.

Proctor, Samuel D. *The Certain Sound of the Trumpet: Crafting a Sermon of Authority*. King of Prussia, PA: Judson, 1994.

Putnam, Robert D. *Bowling Alone: The Collapse and Revival of American Community*. New York: Touchstone, 2001.

Rah, Soong-Chan. *Prophetic Lament: A Call for Justice in Troubled Times*. Downers Grove, IL: InterVarsity, 2015.

Ritzger, Roger. *The McDonaldization of Society: An Investigation into the Changing Character of Contemporary Social Life.* 6th ed. Thousand Oaks, CA: Pine Forge, 1993.

Robinson, Stephen A. *Mega-Small Church: Making Big Things Small.* St. Petersburg, FL: Book Locker, 2017.

Roxburgh, Alan. "Reclaiming the Commons: What It Is and Why It's Important." *Journal of Missional Practice* (Spring 2016). http://journalofmissionalpractice.com/reclaiming-the-commons/.

Salter McNeil, Brenda. *Roadmap to Reconciliation: Moving Communities into Unity, Wholeness and Justice.* Downers Grove, IL: InterVarsity, 2016.

Saunders, Doug. *Arrival City: How the Largest Migration in History Is Reshaping Our World.* New York: Random House, 2010.

Sexton, James J. *If You're in My Office, It's Already Too Late: A Divorce Lawyer's Guide to Staying Together.* New York: Holt, 2018.

Shapiro, Thomas M. *Toxic Inequality: How America's Wealth Gap Destroys Mobility, Deepens the Racial Divide, and Threatens Our Future.* New York: Basic, 2017.

Sheldrake, Philip. *The Spiritual City: Theology, Spirituality, and the Urban.* Malden, MA: Wiley-Blackwell, 2014.

Smith, James K. A. *You Are What You Love: The Spiritual Power of Habit.* Grand Rapids: Brazos, 2016.

Smith, Noah. "Social Media Looks Like the New Opiate of the Masses." *Bloomberg,* April 4, 2018. https://www.bloomberg.com/view/articles/2018-04-04/social-media-use-bears-similarities-to-drug-addiction.

Snyder, Howard A. *Small Voice, Big City: The Challenge of Urban Mission.* Urban Ministry in the 21st Century 6. Skyforest, CA: Urban Loft, 2016.

———. *Yes in Christ: Wesleyan Reflections on Gospel, Mission, and Culture.* Tyndale Studies in Wesleyan History and Theology 2. Toronto: Clements Academic, 2011.

Solon, Olivia. "Ex-Facebook President Sean Parker: Site Made to Exploit Human 'Vulnerability.'" *Guardian,* November 9, 2017. https://www.theguardian.com/technology/2017/nov/09/facebook-sean-parker-vulnerability-brain-psychology.

Sproul, R. C. *Essential Truths of the Christian Faith.* Wheaton, IL: Tyndale, 1998.

Stevenson, Bryan. *Just Mercy: A Story of Justice and Redemption.* Melbourne: Scribe, 2020.

Stiglitz, Joseph E. *The Great Divide: Unequal Societies and What We Can Do About Them.* New York: Norton, 2016.

Stott, John R. W. *The Cross of Christ.* Rev. ed. Downers Grove, IL: InterVarsity, 2006.

———. *The Message of Ephesians.* The Bible Speaks Today. Downers Grove, IL: InterVarsity, 1989.

———. *The Message Of Romans: God's Good News For The World.* The Bible Speaks Today. Downers Grove, IL: InterVarsity, 2004.

Sunquist, Scott W. *Understanding Christian Mission: Participation in Suffering and Glory.* Grand Rapids: Baker Academic, 2017.

Swanson, Eric, and Sam Williams. *To Transform a City: Whole Church, Whole Gospel, Whole City.* Grand Rapids: Zondervan, 2010.

Taylor, Adam. *Mobilizing Hope: Faith-Inspired Activism for a Post-Civil Rights Generation.* Downers Grove, IL: InterVarsity, 2010.

Tennent, Timothy C. *Invitation to World Missions: A Trinitarian Missiology for the Twenty-first Century.* Invitation to Theological Studies Series. Grand Rapids: Kregel, 2010.

Thiselton, Anthony C. *The Holy Spirit: In Biblical Teaching, through the Centuries and Today.* Grand Rapids: Eerdmans, 2013.

Thompson, Derek. "Craft Beer Is the Strangest, Happiest Economic Story in America." *Atlantic*, January 19, 2018. https://www.theatlantic.com/business/archive/2018/01/craft-beer-industry/550850/.

Tisby, Jemar. *Color of Compromise: The Truth about the American Church's Complicity in Racism*. Grand Rapids: Zondervan, 2020.

Toly, Noah J. "In the City We Trust: Urban Dynamism, Utopian Dreams, and Human Brokeness." *Books & Culture*, 2014. http://www.booksandculture.com/articles/2014/janfeb/in-city-we-trust.html?paging=off.

Twenge, Jean M. "Have Smartphones Destroyed a Generation?" *Atlantic*, September 2017. https://www.theatlantic.com/magazine/archive/2017/09/has-the-smartphone-destroyed-a-generation/534198/.

United Nations. "Report: Majority of trafficking victims are women and girls; one-third children." Sustainable Development Goals. Accessed January 9, 2020. https://www.un.org/sustainabledevelopment/blog/2016/12/report-majority-of-trafficking-victims-are-women-and-girls-one-third-children/.

United States Census Bureau. "U.S. Cities are Home to 62.7 Percent of the U.S. Population, but Comprise Just 3.5 Percent of Land Area." March 4, 2015. https://www.census.gov/newsroom/press-releases/2015/cb15-33.html.

U.S. Embassy & Consulates in Brazil. U.S. Mission Brazil. "Farewell Message by Ambassador McKinley: Partners for a better tomorrow." November 5, 2018. https://br.usembassy.gov/farewell-message-by-ambassador-mckinley-partners-for-a-better-tomorrow/.

Vance, J. D. *Hillbilly Elegy: A Memoir of a Family and Culture in Crisis*. New York: HarperCollins, 2016.

Volf, Miroslav. *After Our Likeness: The Church as the Image of the Trinity*. Sacra Doctrina: Christian Theology for a Postmodern Age. Grand Rapids: Eerdmans, 1998.

———. *Exclusion and Embrace: A Theological Exploration of Identity, Otherness, and Reconciliation*. Rev. ed. Nashville: Abingdon, 2019.

———. *A Public Faith: How Followers of Christ Should Serve the Common Good*. Grand Rapids: Brazos, 2013.

Walt, J. D. *Creed: A Seven-Week Reflection Guide on the Apostles' Creed*. Wilmore, KY: Seedbed, 2012.

Ward, Adrian F., et al. "Brain Drain: The Mere Presence of One's Own Smartphone Reduces Available Cognitive Capacity." *Journal of the Association for Consumer Research* 2, no. 2 (April 2017) 140–54. https://www.journals.uchicago.edu/doi/abs/10.1086/691462.

Warrington, Keith. *The Message of the Holy Spirit*. The Bible Speaks Today. Grand Rapids: InterVarsity, 2009.

Wear, Michael. *Reclaiming Hope: Lessons Learned in the Obama White House About the Future of Faith in America*. Nashville: Thomas Nelson, 2018.

Wong, Julia Carrie. "Former Facebook executive: social media is ripping society apart." *Guardian*, December 12, 2017. https://www.theguardian.com/technology/2017/dec/11/facebook-former-executive-ripping-society-apart.

Woodward, J. R. *Creating a Missional Culture: Equipping the Church for the Sake of the World*. Downers Grove, IL: InterVarsity, 2012.

Woodward, J. R., and Dan White Jr. *The Church as Movement: Starting and Sustaining Missional-Incarnational Communities*. Downers Grove, IL: InterVarsity, 2016.

Wright, Christopher J. H. *The Mission of God: Unlocking the Bible's Grand Narrative*. Downers Grove, IL: InterVarsity, 2006.

Wright, N. T. *Paul for Everyone: 2 Corinthians*. New Testament for Everyone. London: SPCK, 2004.

———. *Surprised by Hope: Rethinking Heaven, The Resurrection, and the Mission of the Church*. New York: HarperCollins, 2018.

Yong, Amos. *The Missiological Spirit: Christian Mission Theology in the Third Millennium Global Context*. Eugene, OR: Cascade, 2014.

———. *Who Is the Holy Spirit? A Walk with the Apostles*. Brewster, MA: Paraclete, 2011.

Zuboff, Shoshana. *The Age of Surveillance Capitalism: The Fight for a Human Future at the New Frontier of Power*. New York: PublicAffairs, 2019.